Peter M. Rinaldi, S.D.B., born near Turin, Italy, first came to know about the Holy Shroud while he served as an altar boy in the Cathedral where the Turin Relic is preserved. A graduate of Fordham University and of the Pontifical Salesian Athenaeum of Turin, Father Rinaldi has studied the Holy Shroud from the day in 1933 when he first saw and examined it. While he was a teacher and then rector of Salesian Schools, he continued to champion the cause of the Holy Shroud with lectures and writings. Published in 1941 by the Salesian Press, his book 'I Saw The Shroud' was the first book on the subject in the United States and sold over 100,000 copies. Father Rinaldi has been a pastor of Corpus Christi Church, Port Chester, N.Y., for the last 20 years and has built a shrine there to 'the Christ of the Holy Shroud'.

14/3L .

£1-5

g

Peter M. Rinaldi, S.D.B.

The Man in the Shroud

A Study of the Shroud of Christ
Originally published under the title
IT IS THE LORD

Futura Publications Limited

A Futura Book

First published in Great Britain in 1974
by Sidgwick & Jackson Ltd.

First Futura Publications edition 1974

First published in the United States in 1972
by Vantage Press, Inc., New York.
© Peter M. Rinaldi, S.D.B. 1972

ISBN 0 8600 7010 7
Printed in Great Britain by
Hazell Watson & Viney Ltd
Aylesbury, Bucks

In profound gratitude for his kindness

To His Majesty
HUMBERT II OF SAVOY

To Whose Family The World Owes
The Preservation Of The Holy Shroud
Through The Centuries

The Disciple Jesus loved said to Peter,
'It is the Lord'.
—John 21, 7

ACKNOWLEDGEMENT

The author's heartfelt appreciation is extended to Miss Marie Prochilo, of Port Chester, N.Y., for her valuable assistance in the production of this work; to the Rev. Adam J. Otterbein, C.SS.R., of the Holy Shroud Guild, Esopus, N.Y., for a critical reading of the manuscript; and to Mrs. Leo Haiblum, of Harrison, N.Y. for facilitating his work. For early and welcome encouragement the author thanks the Rev. Piero Coero Borga and the Rev. Luigi Fossati, of Turin, Italy; and Monsignor Giulio Ricci, of Vatican City. Lastly, a special debt is owed by the author to the clergy and laity of Corpus Christi Parish, Port Chester, N.Y. Their devotion to the cause of the Holy Shroud has been, through many years, a source of inspiration to him.

PREFACE

Not unlike the Crucified Master, His Burial Shroud seems destined to remain a sign of contradiction. To most persons it is simply incredible that a linen cloth should have been preserved for so many centuries; even more incredible that it should bear so exact a negative imprint of the Saviour's Body that its photograph offers the world the actual portrait of Christ. They dismiss, therefore, the whole case without a hearing and regard the defenders of the Shroud as credulous fanatics or interested propagandists.

Yet men of learning and renown have accepted the Shroud as authentic. They are convinced it bears its own evidence for all to see. This is all the more remarkable since the Shroud, though preserved for centuries through Catholic reverence, has not been a major concern of the Church, at least with regard to the scientific investigations since the sensational photographic revelation of 1898.

It has been my privilege to see and examine the Holy Shroud. Like many another pilgrim in Turin, Italy, in the fall of 1933, I found my way again and again to the Cathedral where the Relic was exposed for veneration. With a few privileged ones I was admitted to examine it closely before it was once more returned to its vault on the altar of the Cathedral's Royal Chapel. To me, even as to those who stood or knelt with me within easy reach of the Shroud, that long strip of yellowish cloth told in a language uniquely vivid and impressive the story of the sufferings and death of Christ. For I believed then, and I am more than ever convinced now, that the Saviour did indeed leave on that linen the imprints of His martyred Body, with the marks of the wounds and blood, the last testament of His love.

The reader may not share my enthusiasm. He, too, may be inclined to dismiss the whole thing as some kind of a pious fraud or forgery of well-meaning but credulous people. Let him calmly weigh the evidence. Let him ponder, too, the words of one of America's foremost Shroud experts: "The Shroud of Turin is either the most awesome and instructive relic of Christ in existence—showing us in its dark simplicity how He appeared to men—or it is one of the most ingenious, most unbelievably clever products of the human mind and hand on record. It is one or the other; there is no middle ground."[1]

Peter M. Rinaldi, S.D.B.

CONTENTS

IT IS
THE LORD

A Study of the Shroud
of Christ

CHAPTER ONE

MIRACLE IN THE DARKROOM

In the small attic room of a house in Turin, Italy, Secondo Pia was bending over a tray of chemicals. The room was totally darkened save for a small red lamp. It had been an exciting day for the young photographer. Commissioned by the King to photograph the Holy Shroud, he had spent most of the day at the Cathedral, closer to the famed Relic than he had ever thought of coming, the first man ever to photograph Christ's Burial Cloth, one of Christendom's most venerated objects. He was now developing one of the photographs, anxious to see the results.

Pia peered more deeply into his tray where he had placed the large negative glass plate in a solution of oxolate of iron. He watched the tiny silver particles go sliding off the plate to become dissolved in the solution. Finally, in the dim, red glare, he held the dripping plate before his eyes. A vision? It was all he could think of for a brief moment, for slowly emerging before him, in amazing clearness, was the face of a man, a noble and majestic face,

17

never seen before and yet strangely familiar, the face of the dead Christ.

Were his eyes deceiving him? Had he made a mistake in taking the photograph or developing the plate? Clearly the image on his negative was the positive picture of the Crucified One, exact in every detail and endowed with a marvellous expression. How could it have derived from the blurred, dim imprint visible on the Shroud? Gradually he understood. If the picture on his negative plate was a positive, it could only be because he had photographed a negative.

Incredible as it may have seemed, it was true. It meant that Christ's actual portrait was on the Shroud, though it was there in reverse, exactly as on a negative. By turning the Shroud's negative image into a positive picture, Pia's photograph had revealed the Saviour's Body exactly as it appeared when laid in the sepulchre.

It was the year 1898. The news that an actual photograph of Jesus had been discovered caused a furore throughout Europe. There was attack and rebuttal. Today the proof of authenticity is so much in favour of the Shroud that few dispute it. Learned scientists, particularly noted physicians and anatomists who have examined the Shroud pictures, have found them to be a perfect counterpart of the

Gospel narrative of the Passion and Death of Christ.

The less scientific minded see in the fact of the Shroud image, as revealed by photography, the Relic's strongest claim to authenticity. As they gaze at that incomparable countenance, they ask impatiently: "If it is not Jesus, who, then, can he be?" They know that no artist could have produced it since it is in no way a pictorial portrait. They know, too, that it is unlike anything iconography ever gave the world. Yet that Face is strangely familiar, overpowering, too, in the calm, serene majesty of death. It is no wonder that they stand in awe before it and whisper, "It is the Lord!"

CHAPTER TWO

THE KNOWN HISTORY OF THE HOLY SHROUD

Is it possible for the Burial Sheet of Christ to have been preserved intact for more than nineteen centuries? And, again, is it possible to reconstruct the chain of events that links the Turin Shroud to Christ's burial?

As for the first question, there is really no difficulty in a cloth being preserved for such a long period of time. I have seen in the Egyptian museum of Turin linens well over three thousand years old which are still as new. The Shroud, a closely woven linen fabric, is actually in a good state of preservation, except where it was damaged by fire, as we will see.

As to reconstructing the chain of events that links the Turin Shroud to Calvary, the task is by no means easy. History alone can only prove the fact that the Turin Relic *might* be Christ's own burial cloth, not that it actually is. Other "shrouds" are known to have claimed the same origin. Quite evidently, there can only be one true shroud. This is why the Turin Shroud was destined to be an object of dispute, until science and applied technical skill came to support its claim to authenticity.

The recorded history of the Turin Shroud begins in France in the year 1353. On June 20 of that year, Geoffroy de Charny, Lord of Savoisie and Lirey, founded at Lirey a collegiate church with six canonries, and in this church he exposed for veneration the "true Burial Sheet of Christ."[2]

For more than a century the Shroud remained in the keeping of the Charny family and shared in the vicissitudes of the same. It followed them as their best-loved treasure wherever they went, in Burgundy and in Flanders, everywhere an object of veneration, of dispute and polemics. For in the meantime other "shrouds" had begun to claim veneration in France. Copies were often made, touched to the true Shroud by way of consecrating them, and then kept and revered first as copies, later as originals. Not a few of these copies are still extant. Pictorially, they are pathetic failures, their flaws and painted origin being more than evident.

In 1452, Margaret of Charny, at that time the only survivor of the family and, consequently, the last legitimate owner of the Shroud, took the Relic to the court of Chambéry where she presented it to Ann of Lusignan, wife of Louis, duke of Savoy. From this time the House of Savoy was to own and treasure the Holy Shroud, repeatedly displaying it with papal approval as the "true Shroud of Our Lord" in the Sainte Chapelle, near the ducal palace of Chambéry.

On the night of December 3, 1532, the Holy Shroud narrowly escaped being destroyed by fire. The Duke's blacksmith and two Franciscan friars saved the Relic by pouring buckets of water on the partly melted silver case in which the Cloth was kept carefully folded. We will see to what extent this fire damaged the precious Relic.

A safe and permanent location for the Holy Shroud was not to be found until 1578, when Emmanuel Philbert of Savoy ordered it to Turin, the capital of his states. There the Shroud is still kept, rolled on a wooden staff, in a long, narrow silver chest which is safely stored in the centre of a monumental altar in the magnificent Royal Chapel adjoining the Cathedral.

This, in its main lines, is the recorded history of the Holy Shroud. There are gaps in this history which we cannot hope to fill, particularly during the period that precedes its arrival in Europe. Of this period we have no record by which we might trace the Shroud back to Christ.

It should be noted, however, that scattered documents are extant that prove that the Shroud of Christ was known to exist and to bear the imprints of His Body long before it became Europe's most treasured and most discussed relic. In the year 120, St. Braulio of Seville wrote of it as a then well-known relic. In 670, Arculph, a French bishop, testified that he was present in Jerusalem when the "Lord's Shroud" was taken from a shrine and shown to a multitude of people. He had even been allowed to kiss it. The Preface of the ancient Spanish Liturgy for the Saturday after Easter (dating from the second half of the seventh century) mentions the Shroud of Christ as bearing the imprints of His Body. In the eighth century St. John Damascene listed it with other revered relics. In 1171, Archbishop William of Tyre; in 1201, Nicholas Mesaritas; and, contemporarily, other less noted authors recorded that the Shroud of Christ was kept in the chapel of Our Lady of Blachernes at Constantinople. There, we learn from one of the chroniclers of the Crusades, Robert de Clari, "It was exposed every Friday for all to see, stretched upright, so that all could see the image of the Saviour." He adds: "Neither Greek nor Frenchman knew what happened to that Shroud after the town was taken."[3]

We have seen that in 1353, nearly a century and a half after the French crusaders conquered Constantinople, a "true Shroud of the Lord" appeared at Lirey, France, owned by Geoffroy I de Charny. How had he come into possession of this "shroud"? Whether for reasons of discretion and state policy or simply because Geoffroy had not chosen to reveal it to them, this question was left unanswered by the priests of Lirey in all the series of documents which deal with the opposition they sustained by the Bishops of Troyes, Henri de Poitiers and Pierre d'Arcis.

Many learned students of the Holy Shroud hold that the Lirey (now Turin) Shroud is the same that was venerated in the Church of St. Stephen at Besançon, France, from 1207 to 1349. The fire which in 1349 destroyed that ancient church did not destroy, as had been supposed at first, its most valuable relic, the Burial Sheet of the Redeemer brought from Constantinople by a crusading captain, Otho de la Roche, in 1207. As no trace of the relic was found amid the smouldering ruins of the church, the inference was that it had been destroyed.

That Geoffroy I de Charny should build for his "shroud" a church at Lirey in 1353, only three years after the fire at the Besançon church, seems more than a mere coincidence. However, other students of the Turin Shroud, disregarding its probable identity with the Besançon shroud, prefer to believe with the historian Duchesne[4] that the Lords of Charny obtained the Shroud directly from Constantinople during the campaigns of the Fourth Crusade. Whatever the history of the Shroud prior to its Lirey sojourn, it is certain that the Lirey Shroud was undoubtedly the present Turin Shroud, because its history from this point is both clear and continuous.

It is a curious paradox that whereas eminent scientists, some of whom, like M. Yves Delage, are not even Christian believers, are willing to accept the Shroud as authentic on purely scientific grounds, not a few learned Catholics, led by Ulysses Chevalier and Herbert Thurston, S.J.,[5] persistently opposed this view, basing their opposition solely on historical grounds. But clearly, if the Holy Shroud can supply its own authentication, it is of comparatively small consequence what may have been its history. Now the proofs gathered from the objective examination of the Turin Relic are more that sufficient to warrant its claim to authenticity. This may explain why the opposition that had waxed so strong and relentless during and after the 1898 exposition has quite generally subsided.

CHAPTER THREE

THE HOLY SHROUD AS PILGRIMS SEE IT

What is it pilgrims see when, during the seldom recurring expositions of the famous Relic, they flock by the thousand to the Cathedral of Turin? A long strip of yellowish cloth (14 feet 3 inches long and 3 feet 7 inches wide) variedly marked with stains, burns and patches, forms the great centre of attraction for those eager and reverent eyes. The Cloth is always shown in a frame (Fig. 4) the length of which runs parallel to the ground. The spectators perceive two rather vague imprints of a human body in natural size, placed head to head, outlined in the centre of the linen.

Fig. 4 shows the Shroud exactly as it appears to the more privileged pilgrim who looks at it from the altar steps. The two dark streaks that run parallel to the sides of the Cloth are the traces left by a fire which nearly destroyed the Relic at Chambéry in 1532. At that time, the Shroud, folded eight times lengthwise and four times crosswise, was kept in a silver chest. When the chest was rescued from the flames, one side had already been partly melted. A corner of the folded Shroud was charred where a piece of the red-hot metal had fallen, and the scorching reproduced itself symmetrically through all the several layers of the Cloth. Other stains were made by water poured on to quench the fire. The mended portions are the work of the Chambéry nuns who used altar linen in repairing the precious Cloth.

The burns, patches and water stains, and even the many creases on the Cloth, tend to divert the eye from what should be its great point of attraction: the two shadow-like images in the centre of the Shroud. On the fourteen-foot length of cloth it is not easy for the viewer to grasp and interpret their significance. Photography has made it possible for us to view the Shroud as a whole, at one glance and yet correctly, reducing that long expanse of cloth into small compass. Yet even when seen on photograph these images appear somewhat blurred and formless: they are the imprints of the Body of our Saviour.

Fig. 1 illustrates the manner of burial that made the imprint on the Shroud double, frontal and dorsal. It was a hurried and temporary burial the bereaved disciples tendered their beloved Master. They would come back soon after the great

Paschal Sabbath to complete the operations. And so they laid the martyred Body upon one half of the "clean shroud," and then covered it over with the other half. "So Joseph took the body, wrapped it in a clean shroud . . ." (Mat. 27, 59).

The reader is now invited to examine Fig. 5, a larger photograph of the Shroud as it appears when exposed for veneration. I do not expect him to be impressed to any degree from his study of this picture. Perhaps he may even be disappointed. He may have already thought that those shadow-like imprints constitute no portrait of Jesus at all; that it takes no small effort of the imagination to see in those stains the traits of the Crucified One. This is all very true. The images of the Shroud are both meaningless and disappointing. The detail of the face as seen on the Shroud (Fig. 13) is even more disconcerting; it looks unnatural, expressionless, more like a mask than a face. It is certainly not a portrait.

Let me remind my reader again that on Fig. 5 he sees the Shroud such as pilgrims see it when exposed at the Turin Cathedral and that he is, therefore, experiencing the same disappointment with regard to the imprints. And rightly so, for on the Shroud the images are shown reversed in light and shade and position from what they are in reality. They are a perfect negative, and they look as meaningless and grotesque as would the picture of any one of us on a negative film. We know this because photography gave us the positive version of the Shroud's mysterious imprints, thus revealing to us the true nature and significance of those stains that make the Turin Shroud the most precious cloth in the world.

CHAPTER FOUR

THE HOLY SHROUD AS PHOTOGRAPHY REVEALS IT

We have seen what happened in Secondo Pia's darkroom: the unexpected (cf. p. 17). A positive picture appeared on his negative plate. Normally, when a person or object is photographed, a negative image is produced on the negative film or plate, because the lights and shades of the person or object are registered thereon reversed, darks in the subject being represented by lights and lights by darks. To get a positive image from the negative film, all the photographer does is "print" the film.

In the case of the Shroud, the figures that had been photographed (Fig. 5) were already negatives, i.e. the lights and shades of the images on the Shroud were already reversed. Being reinverted on the negative plate, they appeared there as positive (Fig. 6). Are we to believe that these positives constitute a real photograph? Certainly, and a perfect photograph, since they are a direct result of perfect negatives, the imprint or images on the Shroud. Then we can say that we have a real photograph of Christ? Yes, one that is derived from an actual negative of Christ, a negative twelve feet long—His Body imprints on the Shroud—from which can be developed a life-size photograph of the Face and Figure, back and front, of the Saviour's mangled and lifeless Body.

On this photograph, reduced to but a few inches on Fig. 6, we now centre our attention. The Shroud appears on it as it apppeared on the negative plate before Pia's wondering gaze. The meaningless, shadowy, negative imprints of the Shroud have turned positive. And it is the positive figure of Christ that emerges from the dark background of the Cloth, a figure distinct and exact in every detail, the Face (Fig. 14) endowed with a marvellous expression. Looking at that image, we might almost believe that we have come face to face with Our Lord.

The inversion of the negative imprints is complete both as to lights and shades, and as to positions. Compare Fig. 5 with Fig. 6. Notice that all the darks of the Shroud's imprint (Fig. 5) became light—its lights dark—on the negative plate of which Fig. 6 is a perfect reproduction. The positions have also been reversed by the photographic process. Note, too, that only the images of the Body have turned positive; the Shroud itself, the mended portions, the burns, water stains and creases have, of course, turned negative. Compare also Fig. 7 with Fig. 8, and Fig. 9 with Fig. 10.

On the negative, the likeness of Christ stands revealed as the perfect counterpart of the Gospel story of the Passion. Point for point, it is the visual record of the drama of Calvary of which the sacred pages are the written record. It adds to them not a few moving details which make us realize more than ever the extent of the sufferings of the God-Man.

To the study of these details we will later give more space and attention. In the meantime, the reader who will not lose sight of Fig. 6 (see also Fig. 8 and Fig. 10) may find the following brief comments informative and interesting.

He may have already noticed that the Face which on the Shroud is quite meaningless, being reversed like a negative (Fig. 13), when seen on the photographic negative (Fig. 14), takes on the wondrous expression which has elicited the admiration of countless artists. We see there a reflection of the majesty of the Son of God, a majesty which is both calm and serene even though it is suffused with intense sorrow and pain.

The dark bloodstains from the wounds which stand out so vividly on the Shroud naturally appear white on the photographic negative (Fig. 8). Plainly visible is the bloodstain from the wound in the left wrist (the right hand is partly covered by the left). The reader will likewise note the trickles of blood on both forearms, quite evidently blood that flowed from the pierced wrists, suggesting that the arms of the Crucified One, raised well above the head, did support the weight of the Body. Unquestionably the nails pierced the wrists, not the palms which would have torn under that weight. The Shroud clearly points to this, and does so against all pictorial tradition which invariably places the nail wounds of the hands in the centre of the palms.

The wounds of the feet are strikingly noticeable on the back imprint (Fig. 10), part of the linen having apparently been folded from the heels so that it lay along the bloodstained soles.

The wound of the side is clearly situated on the right, close to a mended portion of the linen. The flow of blood, doctors tell us, is incredibly true to nature. From the position of the wound Dr. P. Barbet of Paris could easily determine the trail of the lance.[6] It penetrated between the fifth and sixth rib, bore through the right lung and pierced the right auricle of the heart.

Again on the back imprint (Fig. 10) where the head rested directly on the cloth, the flow of blood (evidently from the punctures caused by the crown of thorns) left numerous specks or trickles that are as natural as they are unusual. No artist has ever been able to depict this injury in so realistic a way.

The scourge has left trace of its gruesome work over the entire Body, the marks being particularly numerous on the dorsal region. Their shape, number (about 125) and distribution (at random over the Body, but nearly always in clusters of twos or threes) enable us to infer that the Condemned was scourged with little or no regard to the traditional forty legal strokes, and the three thongs of the *flagrum* (scourge) were each provided with knobs of metal or bone. The entire area of the Body, from the neck to the heels, is pelted with lashes, the flesh stripped to the quick.

CHAPTER FIVE

SCIENCE AND THE HOLY SHROUD

The magnificent photographs of the Holy Shroud, made during the Relic's exposition in 1931 and issued with ecclesiastical authority, once again disclosed the astonishing characters of the Shroud's imprints. John Walsh writes:

> As Turin emptied of its two million visitors after the last day of the exposition, the scholars departed armed with copies of the new pictures. A new phase in the study of the Relic was about to dawn, one in which scientists would pile up an impressive body of evidence in the Relic's favour.[7]

Indeed, the Shroud's staunchest defenders are scientists, medical men for the most part. We have mentioned Dr. P. Barbet. "I came to scoff and remained to pray," is the note he sounds in the concluding chapter of his book *A Doctor at Calvary,* an anatomical and experimental study on the figures of the Shroud that won for him the grateful admiration of countless devotees of the Turin Relic.

Dr. Barbet, who will be our guide, points to the realism of the wounds in the Shroud image. The face shows several disfigurements: a swelling at the nose-bridge and on the right cheek, a contusion below the right eye-socket and excoriations on the left cheek, nose and lower lip. The renowned Paris surgeon thinks the realism of these marks is incontrovertible. He is even more certain with regard to the marks left by the scourge. So true to nature are they, so totally different from anything pictorial art has ever given us that he is compelled to conclude: "If these be the work of a forger, he must have been a super-genius as an anatomist, a physiologist and an artist, a genius of such unexcelled quality that he must have been made to order."[8]

Demonstrating first with freshly amputated hands, and then also with a body of a deceased patient at his Paris hospital, Dr. Barbet proved that, in the case of Jesus, crucifixion by nailing through the wrists (as it appears on the Shroud imprints) is the only one the anatomist can reasonably admit. In his experiment, hardly had the cross been raised on which he had "crucified" the dead body through the palms when the nails began to tear through. The X-rays he made of a nail piercing the wrist showed how only the bony structure of the wrist could offer adequate support to the body.

While he was thus experimenting, Dr. Barbet noticed that invariably as he drove the nail through the wrist, the thumb, contracting under the spasm of torn nerves and tendons, jerked and bent toward the palm. This came as an unexpected and welcome solution to a difficulty that had long baffled the students of the Shroud: the absence of the thumbs from the plainly visible hands of the Shroud image. Evidently, the thumbs, contracted in the spasm of the transfixion, became rigid under the palms as *rigor mortis* ensued after the Saviour's death.

The Shroud's dorsal imprint (Fig. 10) shows both feet turned inward, the left knee bent, indicating that the left foot was over the right on the cross, and that one nail pierced both feet at once. The *rigor mortis* kept the feet and legs rigid in that position (cf. p. 78).

The truth-questing fingers of a Thomas could easily have been inserted into the large opening in the Saviour's side. This is the surgeon's conclusion after studying the blood imprint from the wound inflicted by the spear. He claims that the right auricle of the heart, which the spear pierced, could be the only cavity in the Redeemer's Body that still contained blood in some quantity after his death; also that, just before the spear penetrated the heart, water must have flowed forth from the sac of the lacerated pericardium (cf. p. 74).

The wounds inflicted by the crown of thorns are thickest and deepest on the crown of the head. Having become infected, they left on the Shroud many tiny rings of oozing serum, and clots, all plainly visible on the enlarged photographs (Fig. 12). Clearly, the crown of thorns was shaped more like a cap than like the circlet traditional in art.

A mass of excoriations is visible on both shoulder blades, in the outer part of the scapular region. It is particularly large on the left side and suggests the weight and friction of what must have been a heavy, rough beam. Barbet's contention is that Jesus carried only the horizontal beam of the cross part of the way to Calvary. He was forced to carry it, somewhat balanced across His shoulders, walking in a stooping position. It is known that the condemned usually carried only his *patibulum* or cross beam to the place of execution.

The marks of blood on the Shroud, clearly visible on the hand, the side, the feet, the front and back of the head, and across the back of the body—these incredible portraits of clotted blood—are ever a source of wonder to the physiologist who studies the Shroud's imprints. These clots of blood had already partly dried on the surface of the body, and yet they were transferred to the Shroud. Dr. Barbet accounts for this by the fact that the blood which had coagulated on the skin became sufficiently moistened in the dampness that surrounded the Body in the tomb (all the wounds and abrasions with which the Body was covered continued to exude a more or less infected lymph) to form a fairly soft kind of paste which easily stained the cloth. But what astounds him is the unbelievably perfect way in which those blood clots were transferred to the Shroud. It is altogether unthinkable to represent these things in a painting or re-produce them by artificial means. They are so complete and so exact that they may be called "portraits of blood." Dr. Barbet concludes:

I started out with a certain scepticism to examine the images of the Shroud. I was quite ready to deny their authenticity if they disagreed with anatomical truth. But the facts gradually grouped them-selves into a bundle of proofs which carried increasing conviction ... No forger could have portrayed them. Anatomy bears witness to their authenticity in full agreement with the Gospel texts.[9]

To the opponents of the Shroud's authenticity who, on the score of a few doubtful literary documents (cf. p. 54), claimed that the images on the Turin Shroud were merely paintings executed in the middle of the fourteenth century, the scientist has opposed overwhelming evidences gathered from the objective examination of the Relic. These evidences Dr. Arthur S. Barnes has so very tersely and forcefully summed up that, even if in some instances they constitute a repetition of what has already been noted, they will prove interesting and profitable to our reader. Dr. Barnes writes:

There are four reasons each of which could be decisive by itself, and which, taken together, make any further suggestion of painting quite inadmissible They are as follows:

1. The process of painting on a fabric involves the deposit of solid particles of colouring matter upon the threads, so that these latter become partially or entirely hidden. But in the case of the Shroud every thread is visible, and no trace of solid extraneous matter can be detected even by microscopic examination. The threads themselves are

stained more or less throughout, so that the same figures, fainter in colouring but otherwise identical, appear on the other side. Not thus was any human painting done in the fourteenth century, or indeed at any other time.

2. Human work, however minute, necessarily shows outline and shading. It may be so fine as to completely delude the unaided eye, but its nature at once becomes manifest when it is put under the microscope. But these figures have no outline and no trace of shading. The colouring becomes more or less intense by quite imperceptible degrees. The edges fade away into the general fabric so that it is impossible to say where the tint begins and where it ends. That effect is characteristic of natural processes; it is quite unattainable by human effort, at any rate, if unaided by any elaborate mechanical device.

3. In the fourteenth century in France anatomy was not understood, and nothing was known of the circulation of the blood. But here the anatomical detail and proportion is exact, the behaviour of the blood flowing from a wound is true to nature, and the contrast between living and dead blood is duly preserved. Even the characteristic way in which a clot of blood dries, the colouring matter

thicker on the circumference than in the centre, is truly represented on the Shroud, though it takes the microscope to reveal it. But the realism of the fourteenth century was not of this kind; science had not attained to such details of knowledge, nor did men do work that only the microscope could test; the microscope itself had not been invented.

4. The fourth reason carries conviction to the mind even more readily than those three already given. It is that the figures upon the Shroud are shown reversed in light and shade, something after the manner of a photographic negative. If they are photographed they produce upon the plate a positive picture, with light and shade more as we are accustomed to see it. Even the expression upon the face is perfect. But no human being, even now, could paint in this way, not even if he were an expert retoucher of photographs. Such a one might be able to produce a passable representation of a human body in negative, but to preserve so delicate a thing as the expression of a face while thus reversing the light and shade is quite beyond human skill. If that is so even today, when photography has made us familiar with the phenomena of inverted light and shade, how much was it so in

the fourteenth century, when the very idea had not been thought of. Nor, even if it had been possible, could there be any conceivable motive which could have led a painter to work in this way, and make his work so hard to understand.

These four considerations are sufficient to put completely out of court the theory that the Shroud is nothing but a medieval painting. It should never be heard again.[10]

Even among the more learned admirers of the Holy Shroud there are some who would not entirely eliminate the supernatural factor in dealing with this Relic. They see something more than the merely ordinary course of nature in the way God was pleased to leave to the world so striking a memorial of the Passion of His Son. Scientists, however, believe that a natural explanation is possible.

Dr. Paul Vignon, Professor of Biology at the Institut Catholique of Paris, proposed what seemed to many a very plausible solution to this intriguing problem. He said in effect: Give me a colouring substance on the linen which, being thus made susceptible of impression, would act much like the sensitized plate or film in the camera; then give me a fluid which, emanating from the body, would determine a reaction on the linen's colouring substance; and there, simple enough, is my explanation of the Shroud's imprints. He believed he discovered both factors: ammonia vapours in the body which the Shroud enveloped, and aloes (John 19, 39) on the Shroud. He thus framed his "vapourograph" theory which for a time was favoured by many scholars.

Other scientists prefer the "direct contact" theory. They believe that aloes' components and the moisture exuding from the corpse caused the colouring on the linen. Dr. P. Scotti, S.D.B., Dr. Judica-Cordiglia, and Dr. Romanese favour this explanation. Dr. Barbet affirms that the stains of blood on the Shroud cannot be otherwise explained.

But do the Gospel accounts of the Saviour's burial warrant such explanations? It is important that we see what actually did happen on Calvary in the afternoon of that first Good Friday.

"The sabbath was imminent" (Luke 23, 54), and the customary burial ceremonies had to be postponed to the first day after the hallowed period of rest. The fact that the women "returned and prepared spices and ointments" (Luke 23, 56) implies that the Body had not been anointed at all. St. John says that "they wrapped it with the spices in linen cloths, following the Jewish burial custom" (John 19, 40). He does not say that they went through all the usual operations after the manner of the Jewish burials. It is rather arbitrary, then, to infer from that text that the Body was washed, anointed and then carefully wrapped in linens. What would the women carrying "the spices they had prepared" come to the tomb for, early on Sunday morning?

Still unprepared for the definite burial, the Body of the Saviour was laid upon one half of a "clean Shroud" and then covered with the other half drawn over the face (Fig. 1). This shroud, purchased by Joseph of Arimathea on the spur of the moment (Mark 15, 46), had been profusely spread with the spices (a compound of myrrh and aloes ground and mixed together) provided by Nicodemus (John 19, 39).

Joseph thus wrapped the Body in the "clean shroud and put it in his own new tomb" (Matt. 27, 60) there, adds St. John, "since it was the Jewish day of Preparation and the tomb was near at hand" (John 19, 42). It was then but a temporary deposition the disciples provided for the Body of their beloved Master, and this in view of the definite burial they would give it soon after the repose of the great Paschal Sabbath.

Thus do the Gospel narratives set the stage for what has been called the "enigma" of the Holy Shroud. What then, did happen in the silent darkness of the sepulchre?

Dr. Vignon would have us believe that the dissolving urea, present both in the blood and sweat of Jesus' martyred Body, produced abundant ammonia vapours which, in turn, reacted with the aloes on the Shroud, causing the body imprints on the linen. Dr. Romanese, instead, insists that all aloetine (a component of aloes) needed to stain the cloth was the moist atmosphere in which the Body of Christ was bathed as it lay in the Shroud. Both theories have been experimented with some degree of success. But what is one to say of their validity in the specific case of the Shroud?

Obviously, it is impossible to reproduce the conditions of the crucifixion. Once it is granted that images like those on the Shroud may conceivably have been caused by some kind of chemical action, there is little to be gained by further experiment. But it will be well to note that all the four points, mentioned before (cf. p. 41) in order to prove that in the case of the Shroud we are not dealing with any human production, are precisely those which would certainly be present in any such work of nature.

In dealing with the Holy Shroud, must we exclude the supernatural factor?

When we think of the unusual process that has caused the images on the Shroud and consider all the circumstances that were necessary for their production, we cannot but admire the Providence of God who was pleased to leave to the Church and to the world the material document of the Passion and Death of Christ. And if, by a new and no less admirable trait of His Providence, it has pleased Him to reveal to us the figure of the suffering God-Man, it is doubtless in order to call us to a greater and deeper appreciation of His love for us.

CHAPTER SIX

QUESTIONS AND ANSWERS

1. *Is the Holy Shroud mentioned specifically in the Gospels?*

The Synoptics (Matt. 27, 59; Mark 15, 46; Luke 23, 53) speak of a *sindon,* a linen cloth, which all interpreters claim must have been a large cloth, a sheet, well within the dimensions of the Turin Shroud. It is well to note, too, that, according to Mark, this linen cloth was purchased by Joseph of Arimathea on the spur of the moment just prior to the Master's burial. It was, then, an item easily purchasable, intended for burial use and perhaps for other uses as well.

St. John's Gospel does not mention a large cloth, but does not exclude it. The author of the fourth Gospel simply states that "They took the body of Jesus and wrapped it with the spices in linen cloths" (John 19, 40). Besides a shroud, smaller linens were customarily used at burials, such as the bandage or kerchief bound about the face to keep the mouth closed. The hands and feet, too, were usually bound with bandages to keep them in position. Before it was enveloped in the shroud, the body was covered with sweet-smelling substances kept in place with bands of cloth. It would seem logical to infer from what has been said that all John meant to state is that Jesus was honorably, if temporarily, buried in linen.

It is rather arbitrary, therefore, to conclude from the text of the fourth Gospel that no shroud was used, or that it was cut up in strips and used to swathe limbs and body. The burial procedure among the Jews at the time of Christ had little in common with the manner of the Egyptians who wrapped and literally bandaged the body and limbs of their dead with many long, narrow and tightly fitted linen bands. This is certainly not what John intended when he wrote that "They took the body of Jesus and wrapped it with spices in linen cloths, following the Jewish burial custom" (John 19, 40). It would hardly have made sense in any case, since it was a hurried and temporary burial they gave their beloved Master.

We have seen (cf. p. 46) how the bereaved disciples composed the Body of Jesus when they laid Him in the sepulchre. Still unwashed and unanointed, they placed it over one half of the "clean shroud" (Matt. 27, 59) which they had profusely spread with spices; they then brought down the upper half of the cloth over the front. The shroud-enveloped Body was not outwardly bound, as was customary, with linen bands around the legs, waist and neck. These bands were probably placed loose under the shrouded Body in readiness for the definite burial after the repose of the Sabbath.

As for the "soudarion"—"the cloth that had been over His head" (John 20, 7), and which Peter and John saw "rolled up in a place by itself" (John 20, 7) in the tomb at dawn on the first Easter—exegetes of repute (Levesque, Vaccari, Wuenschel, Bernard) believe it to be the shroud itself, the "sindon" mentioned by the other Evangelists. Dr. Levesque writes:

It is well known that the Greek of the author of the fourth Gospel is very Semitic and Aramaic. His diction is replete with Aramaic words. *Soudarion* with him is not, as has been said, of Latin influence (*sudarium,* a sweat-cloth), but of Aramaic influence. The word does not mean a veil used for the face, but a *sindon* or shroud.[11]

Levesque substantiates his assertion quoting pertinent texts. He then adds:

It seems that it was not the custom

51

with the Jews before the destruction of Jerusalem and even after, to use a *sudarium*, a veil with which to cover the face of their dead. It is quite certain that they simply folded the shroud back over the face and down to the feet. This custom is still prevalent in the Orient, at Lebanon, among the original inhabitants of the region.[12]

The writer agrees that the text of St. John should not be "forced" to make it harmonize with the text of the Synoptics or, worse, with the assumption that the Turin Shroud is the authentic burial cloth of Christ. However, it is to the point to note that, whatever the interpretation given to the terms used by the fourth Gospel may be, John's text can in no way be taken to exclude the "linen cloth" in which, according to the Synoptics, Joseph and Nicodemus "wrapped the body" of Jesus, and which, exegetes agree, could well be identified with the Turin Shroud.

2. *Has there been any authoritative pronouncement from the Holy See concerning the authenticity of the Holy Shroud? Somewhere in your study you stated that the Turin Relic has not been "a major concern" of the Church at all.*

The Church has sanctioned the cult of

the Holy Shroud (pontifical acts by Paul II, Sixtus IV and Julius II) and has ever surrounded it with much veneration, particularly during the solemn expositions of the Relic. With the Holy See the authenticity of the Shroud was never an issue *per se.* It was rather taken for granted. Note, too, that the Church's supreme authority placed the seal of approval only on the Turin Shroud, disregarding the claims of other "shrouds".

Recent Popes have shown much personal interest in the studies that followed the Shroud's revelation by photography. Pope Pius XI was a convinced admirer of the Relic and often emphasized the significance of that revelation. Pope Pius XII, in a message to the first International Congress of Studies on the Holy Shroud, held in Rome in 1950, "wished that the participants at the Congress contribute ever more zealously to spreading the knowledge and veneration of so great and sacred a Relic." Pope John XXIII, looking reverently at the Face of the Shroud image, was heard to repeat: "This can only be the Lord's own doing!" Pope Paul VI, in the homily of a Mass in St. Peter's Basilica, June 1967, declared: 'Perhaps only the image from the Holy Shroud reveals to us something of the human and divine personality of Christ."

When I stated that the Holy Shroud has not been a major concern of the Church, I meant that its authenticity, like the authenticity of any relic, is not within the scope of the Church's doctrinal definitions. She leaves it to archaeology and other related sciences. A well-established tradition is all the Church requires to permit the cult of a relic. Unless science can clearly disprove a relic's claim to authenticity, the Church will not interfere. We should remember, too, that (as in the case of images and statues) the cult or veneration is directly intended for the person of Christ or of a given saint, and only indirectly for the relic itself.

3. *What Church authority branded the Shroud as the work of an artist?*

Owing mainly to the researches of Canon U. Chevalier, a series of documents were discovered which clearly proved that in 1389 Pierre D'Arcis, bishop of Troyes, France, appealed to Clement VII, the Avignon Pope (actually anti-pope) to put a stop to the scandals connected with the Shroud at Lirey (now at Turin). It was, the bishop declared, the work of an artist who some years before had confessed to having painted it to his predecessor, Bishop Henri de Poitiers; it was being exhibited by the canons of Lirey in such a way that the populace believed it to be the authentic burial cloth of Jesus Christ.

This memorial of the bishop of Troyes to the antipope is one of thirty-three documents which Canon Chevalier quotes in an erudite work against the Holy Shroud.[13] It is by far the most important in his estimation; and rightly so, for it is the only document which, together with the subsequent unfavourable decision of the antipope Clement, may be invoked against the Holy Shroud. Canon Chevalier attaches a monumental value to this document principally because of the unknown painter's avowal which is nowhere else recounted.

What are we to think of this document? If the Shroud were no longer extant, to defend its authenticity against this document would indeed be a discouraging task. But we have the Shroud, and all its character bears witness to the fact that it is not and cannot be the work of an artist; in fact, that it is not a human production at all.

There are some who have seriously questioned the authenticity of those documents with sound reasons. Without going that far, we should prefer the opinion of those who admit the documents to be genuine but reject the possibility of any such avowal on the part of the would-be artist. No artist could have painted the Turin (then Lirey) Shroud, not even a Michelangelo, let alone some obscure artist in fourteenth century France! It is to some other "shroud" that this avowal must be referred. The complaint of the bishop of Troyes and the unfavourable decision of the antipope are based on the false assumption that the Lirey Shroud was but a pictorial production, one of the many crude and pathetic reproductions of the true Shroud which at that time and even later were quite in vogue in France. It must be noted that none of the documents in question tells of any direct examination of the Lirey Shroud by either Bishop d'Arcis or Antipope Clement.

4. *Do other "shrouds" claim to be authentic?*

We have record of some forty-two "shrouds" which at some time or other claimed authenticity. Some of them appeared in France long before the known history of the Turin Shroud began at Lirey, as the shroud of Compiègne and the one of Cadouin. These linens, brought to Europe by pilgrims, had possibly been laid on the true Shroud at Jerusalem or Constantinople and were later considered to have been in some way connected with the Saviour's burial. None of those that reached Europe before the true Shroud became known in France bore any trace of figures or imprints.

All the painted "shrouds" date back to the time when the Turin Shroud was at Lirey and later at Chambéry. One such shroud was venerated at Besançon from 1350 to 1794. Some believe it to be the one that replaced the true Shroud when the latter supposedly disappeared from the Church of St. Stephen during the fire of 1349 (cf. p. 24). It was ordered to Paris by the French Convention in 1794, formally examined and destroyed. Other notable "shrouds" were venerated in Lierre, Belgium; in Savoy, Piedmont, and other places in Spain and Portugal. They are all without exception copies of the true Shroud, the efforts of the painters to conform to the original being as pathetically evident as they were futile.

In recent times none of these "shrouds" claimed or was given any serious attention. Many of them were disproved and discarded, as, for example, the one of Cadouin which among all others seemed to have some valid claims to authenticity.

5. *It should be possible to determine the authenticity of the Shroud from the material of the cloth and even the type*

-of weave. Has anything been done in this regard? Also, why not use the Radio-carbon test to determine the Shroud's age?

The Holy Shroud is made of linen in a 3 to 1 twill weave, with an overall herringbone pattern in the cloth. Dr. William Geilman, of the University of Mainz, a textile expert, claims that the Turin Shroud is identical in material and weave pattern to numerous fabrics from the Near East, reliably dated from the first to the third century.[14] It is interesting to note that there is no evidence that similar fabrics in the twill weave were known in France in the period before and during the fourteenth-century. Those who contend that the Turin Shroud is the work of a fourteenth-century French artist are thus placed under a serious handicap.[15]

The request to use the Radio-carbon method on the Shroud has been frequently urged on the responsible authorities. It is known that the linen wrappings of the Dead Sea Scroll, for example, were successfully dated with this method, known as the Carbon 14 test. The fabric is tested with a Gieger counter for its content of a certain carbon isotope (C14) which plants are known to absorb as long as they are alive. This carbon is radioactive and its

58

half-life can be determined. It is, therefore, possible to date organic matter on the basis of its content of C14.

There are evident drawbacks connected with this test. First and foremost, a considerable part of the test material must be burned. Besides, experts tell us that, in given circumstances, the margin of possible error is still rather wide, as much as 500 years, plus or minus. In the Shroud's case, some claim that the vicissitudes to which it was subjected through the centuries might even further extend the margin of error. We know, for instance, that in the Chambéry fire in 1532, the folded Relic was extracted substantially damaged from its red-hot, partly melting silver chest (cf. p. 22) after having been drenched with water. As John Walsh remarks, the Shroud certainly "has not enjoyed the undisturbed, airless existence of the Dead Sea Scroll..."[16] With Bulst we conclude that, unless the Carbon 14 method can be further improved and the amount of test material considerably reduced, it is most unlikely that even an appreciable portion of the Shroud will ever be sacrificed for such a test.[17]

6. *What is the actual colour of the Shroud's imprints? What is it that makes them negative?*

The body imprints on the Shroud are of a single colour, a reddish, rust-like dye of unequal intensity. The stains made by the blood from the wounds stand out vividly in marked contrast with the dim, shadow-like imprints of the rest of the body. Actually, the colour of these bloodstains is quite different from that of the body imprints. I recall that I was struck by that difference when I had occasion to examine them directly on the Shroud. I am in full agreement with Dr. Barbet who says that the colour of the bloodstains is the typical colour of dried blood which "had sunk into" the cloth.

What gives the imprints on the Shroud all the characters of a perfect negative is the fact that the reliefs of the enshrouded body caused darker stains on the cloth than the cavities and depressions. We have, therefore, in these imprints a true inversion of lights and shades. Normally, on any object or person the "highs" are well lighted while the "lows" are shaded. In the case of the Shroud's images, the "highs" are dark while the "lows" are light. Hence the typically negative characters of these images.

Finally, let me point out one of the most notable characteristics of the Shroud's images: no trace of solid, extraneous matter can be detected on the brownish vapour tints of these images even by microscopic examination. The threads themselves, stained more or less intensely, are perfectly visible and no solid particle of colouring matter can be traced on them.

7. *Dr. Vignon's "vapourograph" theory supplies the most valid explanation of the origin of the Shroud's mysterious imprints. But why was he so staunchly opposed to the "direct contact" theory?*

Vignon has fully answered this question. He writes:

After analysing the first photographs of the Shroud and making our experiments in our laboratory at the Sorbonne, we concluded that the figures are the direct imprints of a human body. It was obvious at once that they were not produced by mere contact, for contact with the pliable cloth and the irregular surface of a human body would have caused considerable distortion, and there is little or no distortion in these figures. They could have been produced only by the action of vapours given off from the surface of the body, the action being most energetic where the reliefs of the body touched the cloth or were very close to it, less and less energetic at the concavities and the sides, as the distance between the body and the cloth increased.[18]

It is known that Vignon, in later years, began to have second thoughts about his favourite theory. After several experiments, he realized that ammoniacal vapours could not have acted on the aloes as effectively as he had first thought. Such vapours, he discovered, are released by decomposing urea in minimal quantity; probably not enough, in the case of the Shroud, to produce such astounding results.

The writer holds that the "vapourograph" theory and the "direct contact" theory are not mutually exclusive. More experimentation and more careful researches on the Shroud itself may well prove that there are valid elements in both theories. It is quite possible, too, that such researches may lead to new and unexpected conclusions (cf. p. 69).

8. *You seem to imply that, in seeking to solve the baffling problem of the origin of the Shroud's images, experiments were made with some success. What exactly did such experiments prove?*

Dr. Vignon obtained imprints like those

of the Shroud by placing linen cloths treated with aloes over plaster figures soaked with a solution of ammonia. He thus proved that ammonia vapours do act on an aloes-spread linen, a process, he assumed, that could well have taken place in the tomb. We know that the cloth that enshrouded the Body of Jesus was profusely spread with aloes. As to whether sufficient ammonia vapours could be released from the dissolving urea in the Saviour's Body is still a moot question, and, possibly, the weak point in the "vapourograph" theory.

Dr. Judica and Dr. Romanese obtained several markings working directly on corpses. Both of them worked by direct contact. Judica obtained his imprints by spreading blood on the body and impregnating the linen with oil and with essence of terebinth. Romanese sprinkled the body with powdered physiological serum (solution of chloride of sodium) and the linen with powdered aloes. The images obtained in both experiments are in some way similar to the Shroud's imprints, but far indeed from the perfection of the figure of the Shroud.

9. *The imprints on the Shroud are not paintings. But could they not conceivably have been produced by an*

ingenious artist who treated a corpse exactly as is recorded of Christ, and then obtained imprints of it on a large cloth?

This supposition implies a knowledge of chemistry, anatomy and physiology in this would-be artist quite inadmissible in the fourteenth century when the Turin Shroud first appeared in France. The writer has seen the imprints which Dr. Judica and Dr. Romanese obtained directly from corpses. There is nothing in these images of the precision and detail we admire on the Shroud's imprints. The face on the Judica-Romanese images is particularly disappointing, not to say repulsive, far indeed from the impressive countenance of the Shroud's figure.

Can we suppose that a medieval artist could succeed when even now eminent scientists fail in their attempts? The imprints on the Shroud involve principles of science and art which were quite unknown until relatively modern times. Besides, they were the result of unique circumstances which can in no way be reproduced. In this connection, it is interesting to note what Dr. Vignon wrote:

The body could not have been enclosed in the Shroud long enough for decomposition to advance even beyond

Photographs

Clovio, a sixteenth-century artist, depicted the Saviour's burial —as seen on the opposite page—showing how His body's image came to be imprinted—front and back, head to head—on the linen in which it was wrapped. Note the crude reproduction of the Turin Shroud above the scene of the burial. Clovio was familiar with the Relic which he had seen in Turin.

It was not at the foot of the cross, as Clovio would have it, but in the tomb that the bereaved disciples wrapped their Master's body in the shroud. They carried it there in haste "since it was the Jewish day of Preparation and the tomb was near at hand" (John 19, 42). They limited the burial operations to a minimum. Washing, anointing, packing the body thoroughly with aromatic spices, all this they decided to postpone till early the first day after the Sabbath rest (cf. pp. 28–29).

Quickly, then, they placed the body over one half of the shroud which they had profusely spread with spices, "a mixture of myrrh and aloes, weighing about a hundred pounds" (John 19, 39), and then brought down the other half of the cloth over the front. Since it was only a temporary arrangement, the shroud-enveloped body was not outwardly bound around the legs, waist and neck, as customary, with small strips of linen. These and other linens they probably left loose about the body in readiness for the final burial after the Sabbath rest. Luke informs us that the women "took note of the tomb and of the position of the body" (Luke 23, 55), and then left quickly for home where they "prepared spices and ointments. And on the sabbath day they rested, as the Law required" (Luke 23, 56).

As scientists examine the incredible imprints on the Turin Shroud, they ask: How did they come about? What did happen in the silent darkness of the sepulchre? . . . What they speculate has been fully recorded elsewhere in this study (cf. p. 44).

Fig. 1. Joseph who bought a shroud, took Jesus down from the cross, wrapped him in the shroud and laid him in a tomb which had been hewn out of the rock (Mark 16, 46).

For nearly four centuries, Christianity's most prestigious Relic, the Holy Shroud, has been enshrined in the magnificent Royal Chapel behind the chancel of the Cathedral of Turin, Italy. Carefully rolled around a wooden staff in a long, narrow silver chest, the Cloth is safely stored in a vault on a monumental altar over which rises a dome whose architectural style has no equal in Europe.

When in 1578, Emmanuel Philbert, duke of Savoy, ordered the Holy Shroud to Turin from Chambéry, the Relic had been his family's treasured property for well over a century. It had been presented to the Dukes of Savoy in 1452 by Margaret de Charny whose own family had owned the Shroud for over a century.

The recorded history of the Turin Shroud dates back to 1353 when Geoffroy de Charny, Margaret's grandfather, founded at Lirey in Champagne a collegiate church in which he placed "true burial cloth of Jesus Christ," one of many relics the Crusaders had brought from the East. Prior to its Lirey sojourn, the whereabouts of the Shroud are often only a matter of conjecture. Elsewhere in our study (cf. p. 21) we have sought to trace the Turin Relic from Lirey back to Calvary, indeed with scarce success. One thing we do know: the Turin Shroud is undoubtedly the Lirey Shroud. Its history, from the day when it first appeared in the little Lirey church until it was finally laid in the Royal Chapel of Turin's Cathedral, is both clear and continuous.

Fig. 2. The Royal Chapel, adjoining Turin's ancient Cathedral where in 1578, the Holy Shroud, after centuries of vicissitudes, finally found a safe and permanent place.

Public showings of the Holy Shroud since its arrival in Turin in 1578 have been relatively rare. It has been generally and quite properly felt that frequent handling and exposure tend to impair the Cloth. During the last four centuries, the Shroud was displayed for public veneration only twenty times, usually in connection with memorable happenings in the Savoy family which owned and still owns the Relic.

The exposition of 1898 was by far the most eventful since it brought about the sensational revelation of the Shroud's imprints through photography (cf. p. 17) and was followed by disputes and polemics among scholars who argued for and against the Relic's authenticity.

Nearly two million pilgrims venerated the Holy Shroud in 1931, the Relic's first exposition in this century. The technically perfect photographs made during this exposition disclosed once again, and even more dramatically than in 1898, the astonishing characters of the Shroud's image.

In September 1933, the Shroud was again displayed for public viewing in commemoration of the 19th centennial of the Redemption. During the Second World War, a secret and safe refuge was found for the Relic at the Abbey of Montevergine on the Appenine Mountains, near Naples. In June 1969, a private exposition of the Shroud was held in Turin (cf. p. 109) for the purpose of ascertaining its condition and with a view to further testing and research by experts.

Fig. 3. During the public exposition of the Holy Shroud in September 1931, the Relic was carried outside the Turin Cathedral to satisfy the devotion of thousands of pilgrims who were unable to get access into the church.

The pilgrim who came to the Cathedral of Turin to see and venerate the Holy Shroud, his thoughts centred on the Cloth's image of Christ, was often mystified and even disappointed. For what he saw in a huge frame over the altar was a long strip of yellowish cloth variedly marked with stains, burns, patches, water-stains and creases. The viewer was especially distracted by two large dark streaks that ran lengthwise, parallel to the side of the Shroud, with patches clearly visible. These, he was patiently reminded by a guide, were traces left by the fire which nearly destroyed the Relic at Chambéry in 1532 (cf. p. 22).

It was only after straining his eyes somewhat that our pilgrim began to notice two rather vague imprints of a human body, placed head to head, outlined like shadows in the centre of the Cloth. On the thirteen-foot length of the linen it was not easy for him to grasp and interpret their significance. The guide came to his aid once more, asserting that those faint, almost blurred images were actually the imprints of the Lord's Body.

As seen on the Cloth, these faint, rusty-tinted images have no outline or shading whatever. They look like vapour tints that have stained the Shroud, delicately tracing on the linen the contours of an unclad human body. What astounds experts is the incredible precision and correctness of the anatomical and physiological details (cf. p. 72) contained in the faint and delicate tracing of this body. In Pictures 5 and 6, the nature of these imprints will be further explored.

Fig. 4. The Holy Shroud on display in the Cathedral of Turin during the public exposition of 1931.

There is little in this picture that might impress the reader. Like the pilgrim in Turin, he may well experience some disappointment. He knows he must discount the strikingly visible marks left on the Cloth by the Chambéry fire (cf. p. 22): the dark streaks running the length of the linen, the patches and waterstains. . . . But even as he concentrates on the shadow-like imprints of the human body outlined in the centre of the Cloth, he is puzzled. This the image of Jesus? But nothing in these imprints reveals the familiar traits of the Crucified One. They hardly make any sense at all! . . .

Our reader is right. The images on the Shroud are meaningless and disappointing. The detail of the face (Picture 13) is even more disconcerting; it looks unnatural and expressionless. And rightly so, for the figures on the Shroud are *inverted* from what they are in reality. They are shown reversed in light, shade and position, much like a negative. They are in fact negatives. We know this because photography gave us the positive version of these images, revealing the true nature and significance of the Shroud's mysterious stains. The portrait of Christ is indeed on the Shroud, but it is there in reverse. If the reader will compare Picture 5 with Picture 6 (and Picture 13 with Picture 14 for the detail of the face), he will readily perceive the truth of this statement.

For a detailed description of the Shroud, the reader is referred to Chapter 3 of this study.

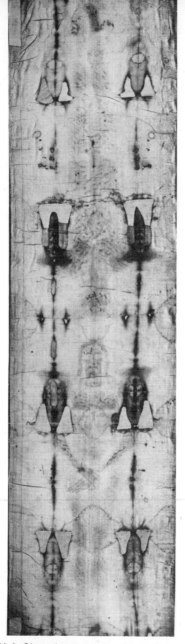

Fig. 5. The Holy Shroud as seen when exposed for veneration.

We have seen that the imprints of the body of the Man of the Shroud are shown inverted on the cloth. They are negatives. Photography proved this in 1898 (cf. p. 18) and again in 1931. The photographic process, reinverting the negative imprints of the cloth into positive images, gave us a true photographic portrait of the Man of Sorrows as He appeared when laid in the sepulchre.

The picture on this page faithfully reproduces the negative of the Shroud's photograph. Let the reader examine this picture. On it, the image of the Man of the Shroud has become positive. Let him compare it with Picture 5. He will note that the inversion from negative (the body imprints in Picture 5) into positive (the body imprints in Picture 6) is complete as to lights, shades and positions. Only the body imprints (negative on the cloth) have turned positive. The linen itself, its singed portions, patches and creases have turned negative as have the bloodstains imprinted on the cloth by direct contact. They are dark on the Shroud and consequently appear light or white on the negative.

But it is especially to the face of the Man of the Shroud that we would direct the reader's attention. Let him compare the face in Picture 5 with the face in Picture 6. Better still, let him compare Picture 13 with Picture 14. It is here that the Shroud's "negative-into-positive" process stands revealed at its best. Can the Man of the Shroud be other than Christ?

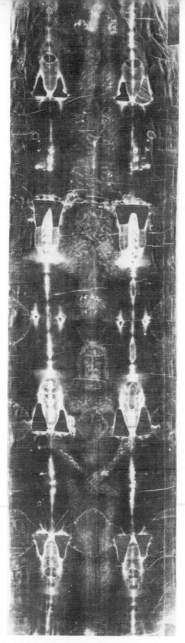

Fig. 6. The Holy Shroud is here shown as it appears on the negative plate or film when photographed.

Fig. 7. A section of Picture 5: the frontal imprint of the Man of the Shroud as it appears on the Cloth.

We know that the image on the Shroud is a negative—its lights, darks and positions are shown reversed from what they are in reality. More difficult to know is how so perfect a negative could have been produced on this ancient Cloth. There are a number of possible explanations by the Shroud's experts which may interest the reader (cf. pp. 44 and 62). While experts may not agree on the origin of the Shroud's image, they exclude categorically the fact that it might be a pictorial production of some sort. They know that these are the imprints of a real human corpse, one who had been crucified (cf. p. 70).

Even only a cursory examination of this picture may persuade the reader to agree with these experts. Note how vividly the blood-stains contrast with the dim vapour-like tints of the body imprints. This is true not only of the plainly visible wound of the hand, of the trickles of blood on both forearms, and of the flow of blood from the wound in the side (near the upper right patch), but also of the trickles of blood that oozed from the punctures of the head, as well as of the bruises and gashes which resulted from the scourging. Treated separately in this study (cf. p. 68) are the conclusions eminent medical men have reached with regard to these wounds and bloodstains.

The anatomical correctness and perfect realism of this corpse in its minutest details is what astounds these experts. "This image is enough proof that nobody has touched the Shroud except the Crucified Himself." Even a sceptic might pause before these words of one of Europe's great surgeons (cf. p. 73).

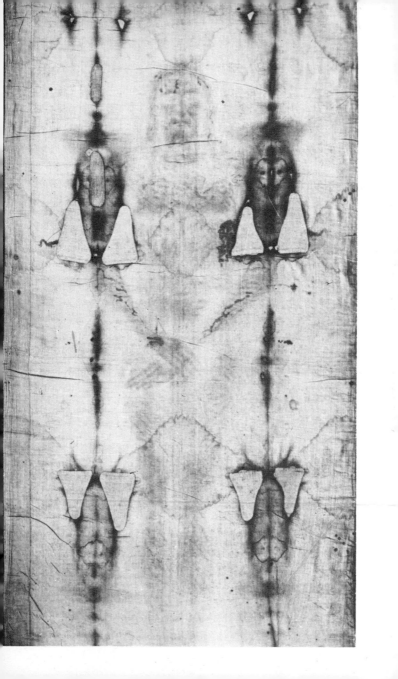

Fig. 8. A section of Picture 6: the frontal image of the Man of the Shroud as it appears on the negative when photographed.

This is actually the image we see on Picture 7, shown here with its lights, shades and positions reinverted into their normal values by the photographic process. The Man of the Shroud appears on this picture as he looked when wrapped in the cloth.

Medical men who examine this photograph detect in it the perfect characteristics of a corpse, above all that of *rigor mortis*. They are certain that the Man of the Shroud died while hanging by the arms. The expanded rib cage and the drawn-in epigastric hollow point to that. It is also evident that he was scourged, and that his head was pierced by many sharp points; that he was nailed through the hands and feet, and lanced in the right side.

The marks of these wounds (rusty-coloured and dark on the cloth) are more easily detected in this picture than in Picture 7 due to the fact that they have been reversed by the photographic process and appear white on the photograph. The reader may have already traced them: the wound on the left wrist (the right wrist is covered by the left hand), the trickles of blood on the forearms and on the forehead, the splotch from the wound in the body's right side. Somewhat fainter are the marks left by the scourges over the entire body. The inferior part of the legs and the feet left a very dim imprint on the frontal part of the Shroud, evidently due to their distance from the surface of the cloth.

For a detailed analysis of the wounds of the Man of the Shroud the reader is referred to pp. 34 and 70 of this study.

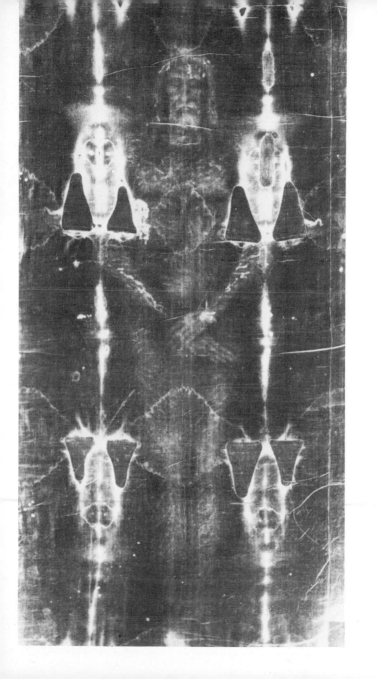

Fig. 9. A section of Picture 5: the dorsal imprint of the Man of the Shroud is here shown as it actually appears on the cloth.

The image of the entire dorsal region, from head to foot, was imprinted on the section of the Shroud on which the body rested when laid in the tomb.

Note the bloodstains on the cloth (top, centre) where the head rested. The scourge marks are visible over the entire body (not excluding the legs), but particularly on the upper dorsal region. Over and across the loins, extending from one patch to the other, may be seen what has been described as a large bloodstain probably caused by blood that issued from the gaping wound in the side when the body was being removed from the cross. The shoulder blades of the Man of the Shroud bear clear evidence of contusions and lacerations left by what might well have been a heavy rough beam. These details will be more fully analysed in Picture 12.

Easily recognizable are the imprints of the feet, especially of the foot at the onlooker's left. A stain outside the area of the sole is apparently due to some still fresh blood that ran down from the wound, coursing sideways on the cloth. Elsewhere in this study we have registered the conclusions medical experts reached with regard to the wounds of the Man of the Shroud (pp. 34 and 70). A question that must certainly plague the opponent of the Shroud's authenticity is this: if this image of Christ is the work of a clever medieval artist, where did he gain the fantastic knowledge of anatomy and physiology so evident in a thousand details in these wounds? Despite decades of efforts, the opponents of the Shroud have not yet succeeded in proving a single violation of the laws of anatomy and physiology in the image of the Shroud (cf. p. 73).

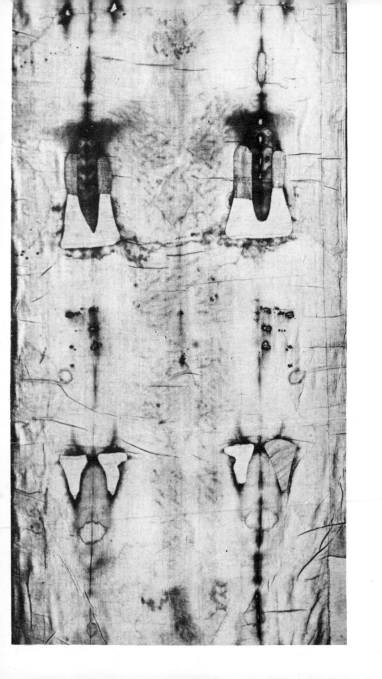

This is actually the image we see in Picture 9, but shown here reinverted into its normal values. The image, negative on the cloth, has been positive via the photographic process.

It is to the imprints of the legs and feet, so strikingly visible on this "positive" of the Shroud's image, that we would direct the reader's attention. They are turned somewhat inward, towards each other, suggesting the position of the feet on the cross. Note, too, how the left leg (on the onlooker's left) appears shorter and bent at the knee. This would imply that the left foot was nailed over the right one, one nail piercing both feet at once.

The reader may wonder why the imprints of the feet appear so well defined on this portion of the Shroud. In the tomb, part of the linen (the end of the section on which the body was laid) must have been folded upwards from the heels so that it lay along the bloodstained soles. Of the left foot only the part around the heel stained the Shroud. It appears that the left leg, being somewhat contracted and bent at the knee, did not allow full contact between the foot and the surface of the sheet.

A point worth making, as we consider the image of the Man of the Shroud, is that it is shown on the cloth entirely naked. Assuming, but by no means granting, that a medieval artist of the 14th century (when the Shroud first appeared in France) did produce this image on the Shroud, how could he have dared to do the unheard of thing—portray a Christ totally naked for public veneration? And we might add: why and how would a medieval artist portray his naked Christ as a *negative* image, an unimaginable conception before the invention of photography?

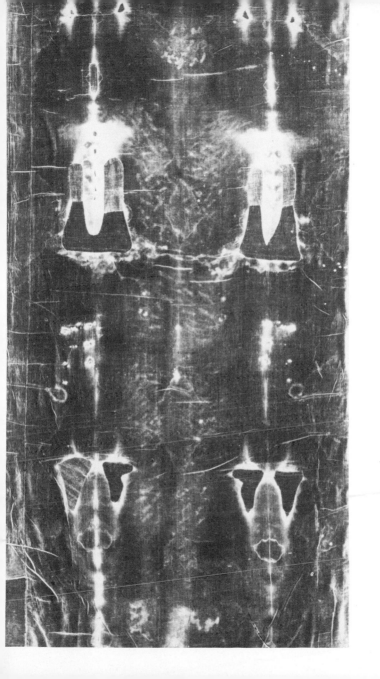

It is in order to assist the reader in further evaluating two of the Shroud's most telling details—the wounds in the wrist and in the side of the Man of the Shroud—that this picture is presented and analysed.

The body imprint is here shown from the neck down to the area just above the knees. Note the clearly visible arms and hands as they cross over the front of the body, the nail wound in the wrist highlighted by a dark trickle of blood issuing from it. The trickles of blood on both forearms, quite evidently blood from the pierced wrists, suggest that the arms of the Crucified One were raised well above the head, supporting the weight of the body. Against all tradition in art, the Shroud's image confirms what was normal procedure in crucifixion, nailing through the wrists and not the palms. The Shroud's medical experts have agreed that crucifixion through the nailed wrists is the only one the anatomist can reasonably admit. They can explain, too, the seemingly odd fact of the missing thumbs in either hand of the Shroud image (cf. p. 38).

The wound in the side, marked by a dark stain of flowing blood, may be seen near the patch on the onlooker's right. As seen on the cloth, this wound appears to be in the left side of the Man of the Shroud, the image being reversed on the cloth. Actually it is in the right side of the chest. Doctors have established the exact location of the wound (between the fifth and sixth rib on the right side) as well as the thrust of the lance into the chest of the Man of the Shroud. They detect in the bloodstain below the wound clear signs of a serous fluid which flowed from the wound with the blood, and are convinced that John's statement in the Gospel, "and immediately there came out blood and water" (John 19, 33), makes perfect sense physiologically (cf. p. 73).

Marks, quite evidently due to the scourging, may also be seen on this section of the frontal image of the Man of the Shroud. They are particularly numerous on the upper part of the chest and on the thighs. The reader is referred to Picture 12 for a more detailed description of these marks.

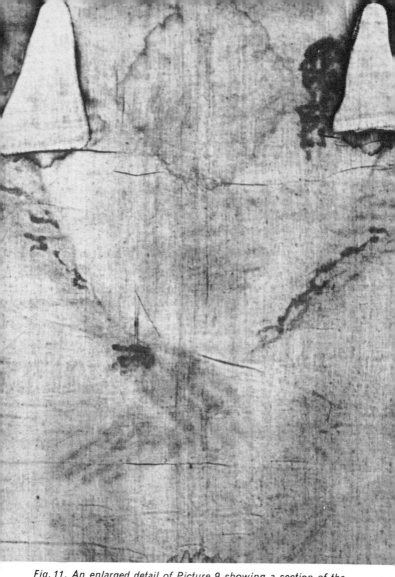

Fig. 11. An enlarged detail of Picture 9 showing a section of the frontal image of the Man of the Shroud as it appears on the Cloth.

The body imprint is here shown from the back of the head down to the lumbar region. Where the head of the Man of the Shroud rested (in the picture: one inch below the top, centre), the flow of blood from the punctures caused by the crown of thorns left numerous specks or trickles that are as natural as they are unusual. Clearly, the wounds inflicted by the thorns were thickest and deepest on the top and back of the head, the crown of thorns being shaped more like a cap than the circlet traditional in art. Having become infected, the wounds left on the Shroud many tiny rings of oozing serum and clots, all plainly visible on the cloth and on the large photographs.

Especially noteworthy on this dorsal view of the Man of the Shroud are the scourge marks. Indeed, the scourge left trace of its gruesome work over the entire body, but it is on the dorsal region that these marks are particularly numerous. The scourge bit through the flesh and left trace of itself in the shape of a tiny double knob. The lashes (about 125) are generally distributed in twos and threes, and appear as if they had been inflicted at random, chance or the caprice of the lictors deciding the direction of the blows (cf. p. 79).

The reader should note, too, the darker areas in the region of the shoulder blades, in the outer part of the scapular region. Medical experts see in them a mass of excoriations, suggesting the weight and friction of what must have been a rough beam. They believe that the Condemned was forced to carry only the horizontal beam of the cross, somewhat balanced across his shoulders.

A little more than an inch from the bottom of the picture, spread across the lumbar region of the Man of the Shroud, is a large stain believed to have been caused by blood that issued from the gaping wound of the heart while the body was removed from the cross. This blood, still fairly fresh and moist when the body was laid on the Shroud, left its trace easily on the linen with an abundance of serum around the marks. For a detailed analysis of the stains of blood on the Shroud, see p. 68 of this study.

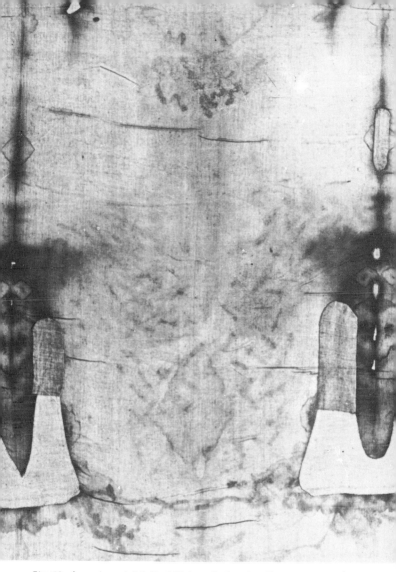

Fig. 12. An enlarged detail of Picture 9 showing the upper dorsal region of the Man of the Shroud as it appears on the Cloth.

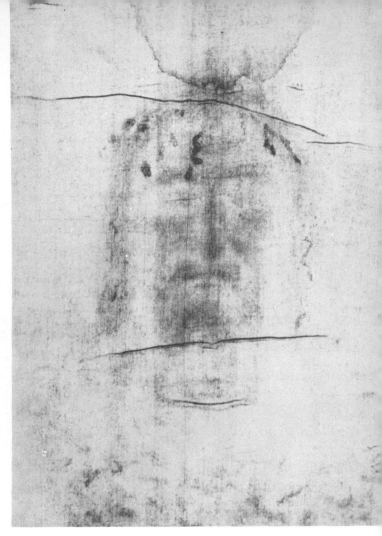

Fig. 13. The Face of the Man of the Shroud as seen on the Cloth of Turin—On the linen the Face, as is the case of the entire Body, appears inverted, like a negative, with no detectable trace of paint or dye. Experts agree that no artist can possibly paint a negative portrait, perfectly reversing lights, shades and positions, and even the expression of a face such as we find on this image. See it now on Figure 14 as it appears when reinverted into its positive values by the photographic process.

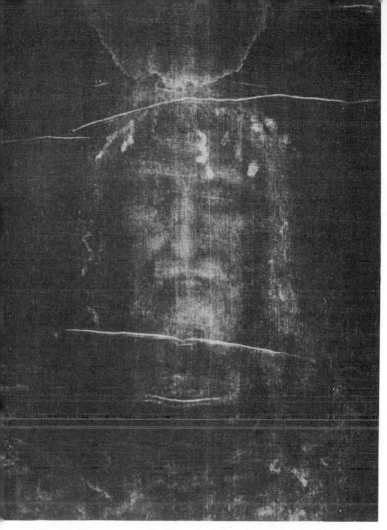

Fig. 14. "It is the Lord!"—This incredible portrait of Christ appears on the negative plate or film when the inverted (negative) image on the Shroud is photographed. It is a positive picture so uniquely perfect that experts find it difficult to believe it is actually on the Shroud, reversed on the Cloth, like a negative. Says artexpert, Dr. C. Viale: "That so incomparable a portrait of Christ should be found *in reverse* on an ancient linen is an enigma to which we art-experts have no solution" (cf. question 19, p. 84).

the first stage, otherwise the imprints would have been destroyed. The Gospels relate that this condition was fulfilled by Christ but only because He rose again about thirty or thirty-five hours after His body was laid in the tomb. In any case, someone would have had to time the Shroud at exactly the right second after all the other conditions were fulfilled, which seems quite impossible.[19]

10. *One would think that the formation of those incredible imprints on the Shroud could be more easily and plausibly explained by courageously, if humbly, admitting that they are the result of a miracle. Why all this theorizing on possible but improbable "natural" explanations?*

Normally God works His wonders not by direct intervention but through secondary causes or, if you prefer, through the agency of natural means. I tend to agree with the scientists who believe there is a natural explanation to the formation of the Shroud's images, but not without the providential concurrence of the unusual circumstances that accompanied the death and resurrection of Christ. In other words, God's Providence was at work over and above the working of purely natural causes.

Others look for a more direct intervention of God. Those imprints, they affirm, were left on the Shroud at the precise moment in which life stirred once more in the martyred Body of Jesus. Geoffrey Ashe offers an interesting theory. He writes:

The Christian Creed has always affirmed that Our Lord underwent an unparalleled transformation in the tomb. His case is exceptional and perhaps here is the key. It is at least intelligible (and has indeed been suggested several times) that the physical change of the Body at the Resurrection may have released a brief and violent burst of some radiation other than heat, perhaps scientifically identifiable, perhaps not, which scorched the Cloth. In this case, the Shroud image is a quasiphotograph of Christ returning to life, produced by a kind of radiance or incandescence analogous to heat in its effects. Hints at some such property are supplied by narratives of the Transfiguration and the blinding of Saul. Also the fact that the bloodstains on the Shroud are positive is now really accounted for. The blood was matter which had ceased to be part of the body and underwent no change at the Resurrection, and therefore did not scorch, but marked the Cloth differently.

Dr. David Willis, from whose study on the Shroud the above has been quoted, rightly concludes:

Perhaps in our present state of knowledge, that is as good an explanation as any. It is consistent with the present conception of matter as forms of energy and the fact of radiation images formed on stone following the dropping of the atomic bomb at Hiroshima. It also ties in with Leo Vala's conviction that the Shroud image is in some way "photographic". Vala is a brilliant, inventive photographer. As an agnostic his conviction is impressive. He writes: "I can prove conclusively that claims calling the Shroud a fake are completely untrue. Even with today's highly advanced photographic resources nobody alive could produce the image—a negative—embodied in the Shroud."[20]

11. *Is there any visible trace of blood on the Shroud?*

Like all who saw and examined the Holy Shroud directly, the writer recalls how vividly the bloodstains from the wounds stood out on the dimly outlined imprints of the Saviour's Body. We have seen how all the wounds are so clearly distinguishable precisely because of the blood spots that accompany these wounds. This is true not only of the plainly visible wound of the hand, of the feet and of the side, but also of the trickles of blood which oozed out from several distinct punctures on the brow and on the back of the head, as well as of the bruises and gashes which resulted from the scourging. The bloodstains are of a dull carmine colour, the ones of the side and the hand being particularly intense.

A great surgeon's mind and eyes scrutinized the Holy Shroud and made it the object of the most intense study and research; Dr. Pierre Barbet. In dealing with the stains of blood on the Shroud, Dr. Barbet immediately calls our attention to the fact that, unlike the negative body imprints, these stains are positive and direct transfers from the Body to the cloth. He then assures us that even a cursory examination of the stains reveals that they were produced by clots, still fresh and moist for the most part. Liquid blood only flowed from the feet in the tomb. Even the large stain across the back of the Body (quite evidently blood that issued from the gaping wound of the heart while the Body was removed from the cross) is due to clots still quite fresh and moist at the time when the Body was laid on the Shroud. "They left their trace very easily," writes Dr. Barbet. "with an abundance of serum around the marks."[21]

How were these stains of blood actually formed? Again to quote Dr. Barbet:

It seems to me quite possible that clots that had become more or less dry, would, without liquefying the fibrin, in a damp atmosphere become sufficiently moistened to form a fairly soft kind of paste. Thus transformed, they would be well able to impregnate the linen with which they came into contact and to leave counterdrawings on it with fairly definite outlines, which would reproduce the shape of the clots. The colour of these drawings would vary in intensity according to the thickness of the clots.[22]

With Dr. Willis we will conclude that nobody studying the blood marks pretends that they admit of a simple explanation. The consensus of opinion, however, is that they are chiefly from blood that has flowed during life, has clotted on the skin, and has been somehow transferred to the cloth. It is Dr. Barbet's firm belief that further study and testing (spectrum analysis is suggested) will undoubtedly confirm the view that blood, human blood, actually did stain the Shroud.[23]

12. *Being a physician, I am keenly interested in the research work which, as you state, has been conducted on the figures of the Holy Shroud from a medical and anatomical standpoint. Are there any further developments to be noted in this regard?*

Let me say at once without fear of contradiction that the Holy Shroud has its most numerous and staunchest defenders among medical men. Werner Bulst, S.J., in his balanced and extremely informative book *The Shroud of Turin*, writes:

> Doctors agree, first of all, on the fundamental proposition that the image on the Cloth of Turin is not an artistic endeavour of any kind, but the imprints of a real human corpse, one who has been crucified.[24]

The anatomical correctness, the perfect realism in minutest details of this corpse is what astonishes medical men as they examine the entire unclad body whose frontal and dorsal imprint can be seen on the Shroud. Again to quote Bulst:

> In all the art of the fourteenth century (to which the opponents assign the Shroud's origin) or in that of the period preceding it, there is no example, either

in the West or East, which can even be remotely compared with the Cloth of Turin.[25]

Among the Shroud's details which not even a present-day artist with the most consummate knowledge of anatomy and physiology could produce, medical men include the following: the perfect characteristics of a corpse in the condition of *rigor mortis*, with the added characteristics of one who died while hanging by the arms, such as the abnormally expanded rib case, the distended lower abdomen, the sharply drawn in epigastric hollow, etc.

Doctors next point to the transfers of blood which are uncannily true to nature, including the separation of serum from the cellular mass. The mark of the wound on the wrist to which we referred at length in our study (cf. p. 37) is against all pictorial tradition. Even the stains of blood from the head, both front and back (evidently caused by the crown of thorns that covered the head like a cap), are so very natural that, upon seeing them for the first time, a practitioner in forensic medicine remarked to me: "These are actual photographs of blood."

I have treated separately the conclusions doctors reached in regard to the marks left by the scourge (cf. p. 79), the wound in the side (cf. p. 73) and also the probable determining cause of the death of the man of the Shroud (cf. p. 76). Those conclusions as well as what I summarized above remarkably confirm the anatomical and physiological correctness of the imprints of the Turin Shroud. To conclude with Bulst: "Despite decades of effort, the opponents of the Cloth have not succeeded in proving a single violation of the laws of physiology and anatomy in the image of the Shroud."[26]

I am convinced that at the forthcoming exposition of the Shroud it will again be the medical men who will say the best if not the last word. Dr. Barbet, after years of intense study and researches on the Shroud's image, believes the medical man has already an overwhelming evidence on which to stake his word. He writes:

I am a surgeon and, as such, well-versed in anatomy which I taught for a long time; I lived for thirteen years in close contact with corpses, and have spent the whole of my career examining the anatomy of the living. The idea that an artist of the fourteenth century could have conceived, let alone painted or stained these negative images is sufficient to disgust any physiologist, any surgeon ... Please, do not even talk of it! This image is enough proof that nobody has touched the Shroud except the Crucified Himself.[27]

13. *It seems hardly possible that from the bloodstain of the wound in the Saviour's side, doctors should deduce such a wealth of particulars concerning the wound and the thrust of the lance that opened it.*

In the early stages of their research on the Shroud, the doctors of both the French and Italian Commission for Studies on the Holy Shroud were amazed at the realism of the wound in the side of the man of the Shroud. There was no question in their mind but that the wound as well as the splotch of blood it left on the Cloth were such as could be caused only by the thrust of a typical Roman lance. The Shroud bears clear marks of this wound on the left side, but since the imprints on the Shroud are reversed, this means that it was on the right.

The text of St. John is simple and direct: "When they came to Jesus, they found he was already dead, and so instead of breaking his legs, one of the soldiers pierced his side with a lance; and immediately there came out blood and water" (John 19, 33-34). It was common practice to break

73

the legs of the crucified in order to hasten his death. His ebbing life was maintained as long as he was able to support himself somewhat on his nailed feet. When this support failed, death followed almost immediately due to orthostatic collapse (cf. p. 77).

We have seen that doctors have been able to establish the exact position of the wound as well as the thrust of the lance into the chest of the man of the Shroud. Demonstrating on corpses, Dr. Barbet showed that the lance penetrated between the fifth and sixth rib on the right side, bore through the right lung, and perforating the pericardium, pierced the right auricle of the heart.

Medical experts are convinced that St. John's words "and immediately there came out blood and water" make perfect sense physiologically. They detect in the bloodstain below the wound clear signs of a serous fluid. Barbet and Judica believed that the blood came from the right auricle of the heart whereas the "water" was clear fluid from the pericardial sac. Dr. Anthony Sava, of New York, proposes a somewhat different explanation. He writes:

The Gospel gives a clear impression that no time elapsed between the piercing of the side and the gush of blood. One might be justified in suspecting that an accumulation of "blood" and "water" was immediately inside the rib cage waiting to be evacuated ... Experience with severe chest injuries has demonstrated that non-penetrating injuries of the chest are capable of producing an accumulation of haemorrhagic fluid in the pleural cavity. It may amount to as much as three pints ... The red blood cells tend to gravitate towards the bottom, while the lighter clearer serum accumulates in the upper half of the collection as a separate contiguous layer ... I submit ... that the brutal scourging of Christ several hours before ... death ... was sufficient to produce a bloody accumulation within the chest so that the settling by this fluid into layers and its ultimate evacuation by opening the chest below the level of separation must inevitably result In the "immediate" flow of "blood" and "water" in that order.[28]

St. John describes the scene as he actually saw it and wants his listeners and readers to believe his every word: "This is the evidence of one who saw it—trustworthy evidence, and he knows he speaks the truth—and he gives it so that you may believe as well" (John 19, 35). The scientist who looks at the Shroud knows that the beloved disciple did indeed speak the truth.

14. *The determining, direct cause of the death of Christ is not clearly stated in your study on the Shroud. Have medical experts come to a definite conclusion on this point?*

Dr. Barbet assumed that the man of the Shroud, because of his position on the cross (suspended by nails in his outstretched wrists with no other support than the nailed feet) must have died of asphyxia, slowly but literally choking to death. This, he claimed, was induced by muscular spasm, progressive rigidity and fixation of the chest in inspiration.

Not convinced that such was the case, Professor H. Mödder, a radiologist of Cologne, conducted a series of experiments on himself and some of his students. Each in turn was suspended from his hands bound to a bar at the approximate angle of crucifixion. If the feet were unsupported, each lost consciousness in six to twelve minutes due to profound lowering of blood pressure. If the feet were supported (as was the case in the Crucified whose feet were nailed, possibly on a rough footrest), the experiment could be maintained much longer, though, of course, not indefinitely. Mödder noticed that the progressive exhaustion and loss of consciousness were not necessarily accompanied by an excessive difficulty in breathing or a choking feeling as might be induced by muscular spasm or rigidity of the chest. He therefore concluded that the determining cause of death is definitely the phenomenon known in medicine as orthostatic collapse, i.e., the pooling of blood in the lower parts of the body due to gravity. In crucifixion death must supervene because heart and brain receive insufficient blood.[29]

Dr. D. Willis favours Mödder's explanation and rightly adds:

Exhaustion from His previous sufferings would account for Christ's early death, whereas the breaking of the legs induced the almost immediate and fatal collapse of the two thieves since the support was transferred from the feet to the hands.[30]

15. *Why are the imprints of the feet so very clearly visible on the dorsal image of the Shroud and altogether invisible on the frontal image? How can you prove that only one nail was driven through both feet at once?*

The blood imprints which the wounds

of the Redeemer's feet caused on the Shroud are very distinct on the back image because, as we explained, part of the linen (the end of the portion on which the Body was laid) was folded from the heels so that it lay along the blood-stained soles and covered the upper part of the feet. Evidently this portion, being spread along the soles, prevented the upper or frontal part of the Shroud from direct contact with the bottom surface of the feet.

We see that the right foot made on the Shroud's dorsal image (Fig. 10) an imprint so well defined it might resemble a footprint on sand. The sole is stained with the blood which, issuing from the large nail wound, flowed towards the extremity of the foot while the Saviour was on the cross. In the tomb, the blood which the extraction of the large nail had caused to flow anew trickled down to the heel and along the folds of the cloth. Of the left foot only the part around the heel has stained the Shroud.

The most notable thing about the footprints is that they are turned inward suggesting the position of the feet on the cross. This would imply that one nail pierced both feet at once. The *rigor mortis,* which followed quickly after the condemned had expired on the cross, kept the Saviour's legs and feet in that position even when the Body was laid in the tomb.

16. *In your study on the Shroud you seem to imply that Jesus was scourged most violently. In Jewish legal procedure, a man was not flogged with more than forty strokes. What makes you reach your conclusion that this procedure was not followed in Jesus' case?*

The Roman lictors scourged Jesus. They were not bound to observe the Jewish law. As we noted (cf. p. 35), the marks of the scourge on the Shroud's imprints are like furrows, visible over the entire body, from the neck down to the heels. They are particularly numerous and distinct on the dorsal region. The scourge bit through the flesh and left trace of itself in the shape of a tiny double knob. Note that, while these lashes are generally distributed in twos or threes, they appear as if they had been inflicted at random, chance or the caprice of the executioners deciding the direction of the blows. Not only can the shape of the Roman *flagrum* or scourge be reconstructed from the size and shape of these furrows, but even the position of the two lictors can be determined.

As to the number of strokes, we need only repeat that Shroud experts calculate that some 125 were inflicted on the man of the Shroud. Giulio Ricci, whose research on the Shroud's imprints has been uniquely precise, concludes that Jesus was scourged the way the Romans scourged foreigners and slaves. Abbé C. Fouard, in his book *The Christ the Son of God,* writes:

The instrument of punishment for foreigners was not the rod of elm-wood reserved for Roman citizens, but a leathern thong, armed with knobs of bone and balls of lead. At every cut from this horrible lash, the skin was raised in ragged furrows, blood streamed forth and frequently the victim would fall flat at the lictors' feet, thereby exposing every portion of his frame to their attacks. It was no rare thing to see the sentenced man succumb under this preliminary torture.[31]

17. *The image on the Shroud shows the nail wound on the hand not through the palm, but through the base of the wrist. Stigmatics from St. Francis of Assisi to Padre Pio bore the stigmata in the palm of their hands. Is not this a contradiction? Besides, did not the Saviour use the word "hands" when speaking to Thomas? "Look, here are my hands" (John 20, 27).*

The outward expression of stigmatization is manifold. The stigmata or wounds are far from being always in the same place and with the same characters in the various stigmatics. As it seems to have been the case with most of them (the first known stigmatic was St. Francis of Assisi), Therese Neumann and Padre Pio had the wounds in the centre of the palm. The wound in the side St. Francis had on the left as did Therese Neumann. Padre Pio had it on the right. It is interesting to note what Therese Neumann herself said with regard to the wound in the hands: "Do you suppose that the Saviour was nailed on the cross through the palms, in the place where I bear the stigmata? Oh, no. These wounds only have a mystical meaning."[32]

F. R. Von Lama in his book *Therese Neumann* discusses at length the phenomenon of stigmatization. He writes:

If one were to make a demand which is theologically untenable—and it has been made—that the stigmata agree absolutely in all respects with the wounds of the Saviour, one would betray a crass misconception of their significance.[33]

Stigmatization in certain privileged souls is not therefore to be considered as a historical documentation of the Passion and Death of Christ, but rather as a manifestation of the stigmatic's profound mystical union with the sufferings of the Redeemer.

As to the word "hands" used by the Saviour in addressing Thomas, it can hardly be taken to imply that the nail wounds were in the centre of the palms rather than on the base of the wrists, as they appear on the Shroud's image. In anatomy as well as in common language usage, the wrist or carpus (in the Saviour's case, the large nail slid through the carpal bones after piercing the tissues) is described as an integral part of the hand.

18. *How did Jesus look? Was He a vigorous man? How tall was He? Does the Shroud reveal these details?*

It does, to an amazing degree. Werner Bulst writes:

The imprint of the Cloth of Turin shows a man of vigorous, well-knit and decidedly virile appearance ... The Jews looked upon a tall figure as the prime requisite of bodily perfection in a male, and a height of four ells (five feet nine and a quarter inches—1·76 m.) was regarded as the norm. The Man on the Cloth of Turin is about five feet eleven inches (1·80 m.) tall. Incomparable is

the majesty and dignity of His countenance despite the torments we can
see He must have borne, in the shock-
ingly graphic evidence in the Cloth.
This is no criminal, no evil-doer. The
radiant repose of death stirs us to the
depths. Artists of note, such as the
sculptor, Professor Hosous, and many
highly educated, believing Christians,
like Professor Carl Muth, the founder of
Hochland, and Paul Claudel were en-
thralled by the majesty of this face.[34]

It must be stated that, with regard to the
stature of the man of the Shroud, experts
differ considerably. Luigi Fossati, S.D.B.,
of Turin, one of the Shroud's keenest
students, writes:

> The Body which came in contact with
> the Shroud was far from being in nor-
> mal condition. Easily noticeable, for in-
> stance, are the abnormally extended rib
> cage, the sharply drawn in epigastric
> hollow, the over extended right leg
> while the left is bent at the knee
> ... Besides, we must take into account
> the expansion of the Cloth through the
> centuries ... Clearly, then, it is wrong
> to assume that, since the body imprint
> on the Cloth is perfect, all one need do
> is measure it and thus obtain the exact
> stature of the Man of the Shroud.[35]

Fossati notes that the height of the man of the Shroud has been variedly calculated from five feet four inches to as much as six feet. He himself favours a high stature. Monsignor Giulio Ricci, a respected archivist at the Vatican and a great sindonological scholar, in his book *L'Uomo Della Sindone E' Gesu'* (The Man of the Shroud is Jesus), by far the best work on the Shroud since Vignon's *The Shroud of Christ,* estimates that Jesus could not be more than five feet four inches tall, a "normal" stature for a Palestinian of Christ's era.[36] Regardless of their opinions on the stature of the man of the Shroud, all students of the Turin Relic agree that only a uniquely proportioned and anatomically perfect body could have left those imprints on the Shroud.

19. *Is there anything in the history of pictorial art that might compare with the Shroud's unique portrait of Christ? What do art experts think of it? Have artists tried to duplicate it?*

The last question might be best answered first. Two artists of renown, Reffo and Cussetti, of Turin, made replicas of the Shroud working directly from the Cloth, during the 1898 exposition. So skilfully did they portray the Shroud's imprints that, looking at them, one might believe he is actually looking at the Shroud. When photographed, the positive version of these painted imprints was a complete disappointment. The images on the photographic negative appear so distorted as to be barely recognizable. The face is a blur. This would lead us to conclude that even a skilled artist, with our present-day knowledge of positive and negative, cannot produce a representation of the human body in negative, particularly of the face, preserving on it so delicate a thing as the expression while reversing its lights, shades and positions.

Dr. C. Viale, director of the Civic Museums of Turin and a leading art expert in Italy, remarks that not only was it impossible for any medieval artist to conceive and execute in negative the figures on the Shroud, but that "these images do not in the least betray a pictorial style proper of any period or school of art, least of all of the time and place in which the Shroud was supposedly produced."

In the fourteenth century, France did not have a school of painters. Gothic art prevailed and found expression in sculpture and stained glass windows. The very few pictorial productions of the time bear very striking Gothic characters. They lack naturalness and realism, the anatomical details are pathetically primitive and disproportioned, the technique is poor and slavishly subservient to older pictorial traditions. Besides, the fact that on the Shroud fabric there is no trace of solid particles and no detectable trace of brushwork is in itself conclusive for the art student: The Shroud figures are not paintings at all.

Dr. Viale concludes:

In all my years of experience with pictorial productions I have yet to see anything that approximates the images on the Shroud. That so incomparable a portrait of Christ with no visible trace of paint should be found *in reverse* on an ancient cloth is an enigma to which we art experts do not have a solution.[37]

20. *It has often been stated that the enigma of the Holy Shroud has been solved by photography. Does this mean that photography alone can establish the authenticity of the Turin Relic?*

Photography's revelation of the Holy Shroud is in the fact that it revealed that the figures on the Cloth are very exact negatives. This disposes, as we have seen, of the theory that would regard the Shroud's imprints as some kind of pictorial production of the fourteenth century when the documented history of the Turin

Relic begins. The concept of a negative became known only through the invention of photography in the nineteenth century. No artist of any earlier period could have conceived the idea of producing a picture in negative.

But photography revealed other astonishing things of the Shroud. By reinverting the lights and shades of the Cloth's negative imprints into their normal values, the photographic process gave us a true photographic portrait of the Body the Cloth enshrouded. That this body can only be the Body of Christ is the inference of learned scientists, particularly of noted physicians and anatomists who have examined and studied the figures of the Shroud as photography reveals them. They have marvelled at the natural and anatomically perfect proportions of the Body, with its true perspective and with a wealth of details whose fidelity to nature is unsurpassed. These scientists have found the images of the Shroud to be a perfect counterpart of the Gospel narrative of the Passion and Death of Christ. They know that the combination of circumstances and even of apparent accidentals which accompanied the death of the Redeemer could not be imagined or effected in any other case. And they confess that these circumstances and apparent accidentals are the very ones, the only ones that could produce the imprints on the Shroud.

We might say that photography has unlocked the secret of the Shroud. On the basis of this revelation, the scientist, the archaeologist and the artist have conducted their own researches, and their findings constitute in themselves very definite proofs of the Shroud's authenticity. Dr. Vignon who, seconded by learned professors of the Sorbonne University, led the way in the study and experimental research work on the Shroud during nearly forty years, sums up the scientist's viewpoint in these words:

> The data of the Shroud, with the Gospels as a key, are a means of identification as sure as a photograph or a set of fingerprints.[38]

21. *Have other than "official" photographs ever been made of the Turin Shroud? Is it true that the Relic's most recent photographs date back to 1931? Can photographs be an adequate, reliable medium for any real scienic study?*

Pilgrims by the hundreds photographed the Holy Shroud during the 1931 and 1933 public expositions of the Relic. It is hardly necessary to say that the results of their photographs showed exactly what the "official" ones had shown: the image on the Shroud turned positive on their negatives.

The Holy Shroud's only official photographs were made in 1898 and 1931. In 1898, Secondo Pia, an amateur Turin photographer of renown, was authorized by King Humbert I of Savoy to photograph the Shroud for the first time in its history. Pia's photographs, as we have seen (cf. p. 17), revealed the "secret" of the Shroud. Giuseppe Enrie, Turin's best known professional photographer, was chosen to make the new official photographs at the 1931 exposition. His photographs have been the basis of all research work done on the Shroud since 1931. Unquestionably, the technical perfection of these photographs can hardly be surpassed in the field of black and white photography. They are the ones used in this study.

The Holy Shroud was again "officially" photographed in June, 1969, during the course of a private examination of the Relic. It is known that colour photographs were made as well as black and white. These photographs which Turin's Cardinal-Archbishop termed "of great interest," have not to date (August, 1973) been released to the public.

To the question: "Are photographs a

reliable medium for any real scientific study?" here is Werner Bulst's reply:

... Photography is one of the most important tools of investigation used by modern science to approach an object. For photography reproduces an object, in the realm of the visible world, with strict fidelity to nature. In the case of a practically two-dimensional object, like a cloth, the object stands out all the more perfectly in a photograph. Furthermore, photography makes it possible to see much that cannot be detected at all by the human eye, through enlargement, intensification of contrast, use of colour filters and properly sensitized film or plates ... Concerning the validity of scientific investigation based on photographs, the author has repeatedly questioned specialists, particularly in the fields of forensic medicine and chemistry, the fields of the history of textiles and art, and in every instance this procedure has received unequivocal approval.

In fact, forensic medicine, which has something vital to say on the possible authenticity of the Cloth of Turin, makes extensive use of photographs nowadays and precisely by this very means settles a high percentage of its cases. But rarely does it have at its disposal photographs of the size and quality taken by Enrie....

It stands to reason that we cannot make a direct chemical study on the basis of the photographs alone; still the optical image of certain substances, particularly in the case of organic ones, is in many ways so unequivocal that conclusions can be reached about the substance under examination. This applies to blood especially, and, above all, to the separation of blood clot and serum...

No one doubts that there are other ways of studying the Cloth of Turin, over and above photography. In fact, those scholars who on the basis of their researches to date have been defenders of the Cloth, have had for some years now a quite adequate programme for further investigation. Regrettably it has not been possible to carry this out. But the unfinished business of further investigation obviously does not make worthless the researches so far made.[39]

22. *It is said that there are experts in iconography who believe that the image on the Shroud may have served as the original model for the early*

*representations of Christ in the East.
Is this possible?*

There is no denying the fact that the
image on the Shroud has many points of
contact with the style of portraying Christ
in the East in the early centuries of Christianity. What is even more striking is that,
in those early centuries, mention is often
made of Christ "achiropoeton", i.e. "not
made with hands", believed to have origin-
ated through physical contact of a cloth
with the Face of Christ. In these early
portraits, Christ's Face is marked by
strong, rather long features, with a virile
nose, deep-set eyes and well-pronounced
arched eyebrows. The face is moderately
bearded, the beard somewhat parted,
while the long hair frames the face, reach-
ing down to the shoulders. The Shroud
image, as seen on the Shroud in its negative version, does agree with this typical
representation of Jesus, at least in its
basic features.

Students of the Turin Relic (Vignon
first among them) have asked whether the
tradition of the "achiropoeton" may not
link them to the Shroud, known and venerated for centuries first in Jerusalem and
later in Constantinople. Is it not possible,
they speculate, that the Face on the
Shroud may be the prototype, the original

model for such pictures? Among these, by far the most famous was the icon of Edessa. Veronica's picture (in Rome since the twelfth century) was one of them, too, as were other highly venerated, typically Byzantine icons.

Wuenschel and Sanhurst support Vignon, and believe that the Turin Shroud actually gave origin to the Byzantine Christ which, in turn, remained the "source" or progenitor of the traditional likeness of Jesus in every school of art down through the centuries to the present day. To prove this, they point to a number of peculiarities or disfigurements with which the artists of the early Byzantine pictures felt compelled to adorn their icons of Christ. All these peculiarities are strikingly found in the Turin Shroud, produced by wounds or bruises, or by faults in the linen, or simply due to the fact that the death mask of the Shroud is a negative.

Maurus Green, O.S.B., in his excellent study "Enshrouded in Silence," after a lucid presentation of the facts that give support to this theory, adds:

A most striking confirmation of this theory can be experienced by the reader. Let him show a *positive* photograph of the Face of the Shroud to someone who has never seen it or heard of the Shroud, and ask him whose image it is. He will get only one answer. The only explanation I can see for this recurring phenomenon is that the ancient artists, who copied the *negative* of the Shroud and gave us our traditional Christ, did their job so well that, when the camera revealed the secret of its mysterious mask, the resemblance was obvious.[40]

Is there validity to this theory? More abundant evidence may be required to support it. In the meantime the mere possibility that the Shroud may have actually been the one and only "achiropoeton" (not-made-with-hands) image, on which successive icons were modelled, is a welcome challenge to both friends and opponents of the Turin Relic.

23. *Miracles are often mentioned in connection with sacred relics. What about miracles through the Holy Shroud? Do we have a record of at least some extraordinary happenings that might be connected with this famous Relic?*

Relics do not cause miracles. Faith is a miracle's essential ingredient. Both the Old and the New Testament Scriptures are filled with miraculous facts in which faith always plays the essential part. "Your faith has restored you to health," Jesus said to the woman who with humble faith had touched the tassel of the Master's cloak (Matt. 9, 22). There were literally hundreds of persons pressing around Jesus on that occasion and physically in contact with Him. Yet only she was favoured with a miracle.

It would be rash to assert that miracles are things of the past, or exaggerated tales of favours granted to credulous people. Lourdes is a present-day fact, and so are other well-documented miracles.

There have been no extraordinary events or miracles connected with the veneration of the Shroud in recent years. There is record of "graces and favours" received by people who knelt devoutly in prayer before the altar of the Turin Relic. On a wall not far from the Shroud Chapel, is a bronze plaque commemorating the fact that, in 1692, Turin was spared from the black plague after prayers were offered at the shrine and a vow made by the town's officials, the clergy and the people. Some believe that the preservation of the Relic from total destruction in the fire of Chambéry (cf. p. 22) was itself a miracle, especially when one considers that the fire, which substantially damaged the Cloth, barely touched the Shroud's mysterious imprints of the Saviour's Body.

In a sense, the Shroud is itself a

"miracle". It hardly needs other miracles to substantiate its claim to authenticity. It bears its own evidence for all to see. There is in the Holy Face, revealed by photography, a mysterious power and majesty, above all petty controversies, that leads one to confess: Truly this is the image of Christ, the Son of the living God.

24. *In your study and lectures on the Shroud you occasionally refer to "responsible authorities". Who are they? Who owns the Holy Shroud? Why do they seem reluctant to take action or even to speak openly on matters pertaining to the Shroud?*

The Holy Shroud has belonged to the Savoy family, formerly the reigning house of Italy, since 1452 (cf. p. 22). It is their private property. No one, least of all the Church, has ever impugned their right to own it. As a matter of fact, the Church is grateful to the House of Savoy for the care with which it has preserved the Shroud through the centuries. Nominally, at least, the Relic is in the keeping of the Archdiocese of Turin, Italy, where it is kept in a vault on a monumental altar in the magnificent Royal Chapel adjoining the ancient Cathedral.

Humbert II of Savoy, until 1945 King of

Italy and since then exiled in Portugal, as the titled owner of the Shroud, could dispose of it at will. He has first word on whatever might be done with it. If it is a public exposition or a private examination that is asked for the Relic, Humbert must authorize it first, even if the request comes from the Pope. From my personal dealings with the King, I can say that he is most willing to act in concert with the Church authorities in all matters concerning the Shroud.

The Archbishop of Turin is the official custodian of the Holy Shroud. With the consent of Humbert of Savoy, he may take whatever initiative he will judge opportune always, of course, with the approval of the Pope. Thus, the present Archbishop, Michele Cardinal Pellegrino, promoted recently a private examination of the Shroud, the primary purpose of which, he stated later, was to observe the condition of the Relic. It was held on June 16, 17 and 18, 1969.

There is no denying the fact that the "responsible authorities" have been slow, even reluctant to take action and even to speak on anything concerning the Shroud. For years, students of the Relic have requested permission to examine it. Practically all research work done since 1931 has been done solely on the official photographs made by Giuseppe Enrie that year. Experts have requested further tests for the Shroud, such as colour and X-ray pictures, and direct testing of the Relic itself. To no avail. John Walsh believes he can explain this attitude. He writes:

For some, this attitude is incomprehensible at best, and at worst it points to a fear of what might be disclosed. The truth is, however, that this problem of physical testing is not a simple one. The Shroud is, after all, a spiritual object, hallowed by the prayers and devotion of many millions of pilgrims, and by the veneration of Popes and saints. Its true value is religious and, if authentic, it goes far beyond even such archaeological wonders as the Rosetta Stone or the clay tablets of Nineveh. Those who have inherited the task of safeguarding it and preserving it into the future feel their obligation heavily. They are understandably slow to endanger even the smallest fragment of it.[41]

These remarks are both well-reasoned and kind, but they hardly justify the "iron curtain of silence" some responsible authorities have clamped down on the Shroud. Among these authorities the jealous or timid custodians of the Shroud's citadel in Turin are unquestionably the ones who, for reasons best known to themselves, have consistently delayed the progress of the Shroud's cause.

25. *Who is Kurt Berna? What does he mean when he claims that, if the Turin Shroud proves anything, it proves only that Christ never died on the cross, that He was alive when buried, etc.?*

Charitably we will say that Kurt Berna, a rather odd individual, is a strange propagandist, who refers to himself as "Dr. Kurt Berna", "Professor Berna", "the President of the International Foundation of the Holy Shroud", etc. The truth is that Kurt Berna's real name is Hans Naber. Reban is the name he uses in England. He claims that he was granted revelations of Christ. In his book *Inquest on Jesus Christ* he details his revelations and expounds his fantastic theories. He is a moneyed man, since he is known to have spent thousands of dollars tirelessly spreading his message, sending out press communiqués to every country in the world.

Berna is obsessed with the notion that Christ did not die on the cross and that it was His living Body that lay enshrouded in the tomb. He claims the bloodied imprints on the Shroud prove this, since blood will simply not flow from a corpse, a totally erroneous assumption in any case. He believes this "world-shaking idea can bring Jew and Christian together, since they would be no longer separated by the insuperable barrier of Christ's death".

Inquest on Jesus Christ sold all over Europe. The publisher's blurb on the English edition describes the book as "a brilliant investigation into the medical circumstances that surrounded the crucifixion and resurrection. The author probes the new evidence and proves that the heart of Jesus was still beating ten minutes after He was taken down from the cross. The author, *who is the world's foremost authority on the Shroud*, (sic) was in 1964 nominated President of the International Foundation of the Holy Shroud established in Zurich ... " Only an expert could set the record straight.

An expert did. Dr. David Willis, England's leading medical authority on the Holy Shroud, in a lucid, trenchant article, published in the *Ampleforth Journal* in the spring of 1969, deflated Berna's (or Reban's) visionary theories and exposed his medical and scientific "howlers".

But the world press is Berna's favourite weapon. He used it to the hilt in May 1969 when the secret of an impending examination of the Holy Shroud leaked out to him. He flooded the press with communiqués denouncing the secret examination as a "plot" to destroy the Shroud and with it the evidence that Christ did not die on the cross. The Vatican felt compelled to inform the press that there was no substance to Berna's accusation and that the Church authorities "had no intention of taking up the question of the Shroud now".

But the damage had been done. For reasons best known to themselves, the Church authorities in Turin made no official statement on the "secret" investigation which had actually taken place in June. When finally they did release a brief communiqué on the Relic's examination, it was much too late. For in the meantime Berna had every opportunity to exploit to his advantage the badly kept secret of the investigation. Thus it was that Berna involved not only the world press, but the Church authorities in the fantasy.

CHAPTER SEVEN

"WE SHOULD LIKE TO SEE JESUS"
(John 12, 21)

Believers in the authenticity of the Holy Shroud are patient and long-suffering. Through now many years, they have hoped against hope that their precious Relic might yet see the light of day and be submitted to direct examination and testing. They are convinced that such testing can have but one outcome: it will not only corroborate the many facts already established, but will also add new evidence to the Relic's claim to authenticity.

Resolutions to that effect were adopted at the two major conventions, of 1939 in Turin, and of 1950 in Rome. From seminars held in many parts of the world as well as from individual scholars, the plea "We should like to see Jesus" (John 12, 21) has been sent out repeatedly to the responsible authorities. But except for polite, evasive replies, the official silence that closed in on the Shroud following the last public exposition of the Relic in 1933, was not broken until quite recently when circumstances practically forced the hand of the authorities. Here are the facts.

In the summer of 1969, the stolid if hopeful patience of thousands of devout admirers of the Turin Relic was severely jolted by headlines that exploded in major dailies all over the world: *Shroud's Claim Challenges Vatican—Christ Was Alive When Buried—Vatican Deceit About Shroud Denounced,* etc. The villain in the story was Kurt Berna (cf. p. 99), but what disturbed the friends of the Shroud were not so much Berna's fantastic claims as the fact that he connected them with a "secret" examination of the Relic held in June. Why the secrecy, why the silence from the Turin Church officials when both secrecy and silence were evidently playing into Berna's hands?

The following letter, addressed to the editor of Turin's Catholic weekly *Il Nostro Tempo* and dated January 22, 1970, expressed the feelings of a great many friends of the Holy Shroud.

Dear Sir:

Major dailies in the United States and England recently reported that the Holy Shroud had been "secretly" examined during the month of June, 1969. In nearly every instance, the newspapers made references to the theory on the Shroud widely disseminated by Kurt Berna of Switzerland. Berna holds that the "Church authorities want the Holy Shroud destroyed since the Relic whose authenticity is well established, irrefutably proves that Christ did not die on the cross, that He was removed alive from the tomb, etc." With this, Berna concludes that the Christian "dream" of the Redemption is forever disposed of.

We deplore the fact that this totally groundless and unwarranted theory should have been linked with the press reports of an "official examination" of the Shroud, causing doubts and confusion in the readers' minds. We particularly deplore the fact that the responsible authorities in Turin failed to inform the press officially on the purpose and outcome of the June investigation.

Regretfully it must be said that the cause of Christianity's greatest relic has for years suffered by the difficult-to-understand reluctance on the part of the Church authorities to act or even speak on the subject. If not actually obstructive, theirs have been dilatory tactics that are perplexing and exasperating to serious students and devout admirers of the Holy Shroud throughout the world. This is all the more to be deplored since Humbert of Savoy, the owner of the Relic has, clearly and repeatedly stated that he is agreeable to a scientific examination of the Shroud provided that the Church authorities will take the initiative.

Will the day ever come when these responsible authorities will realize that the Turin Shroud, in a broad sense, belongs to all of Christianity, in fact, to humanity itself? How can a Relic of such tremendous significance be kept locked and sealed for decades at a time? And when finally brought to light, why is it examined secretly, without the competent authorities as much as issuing an official statement that would obviate the confusing reports of the press releases?

The Holy Shroud Guild in the United States numbers outstanding experts among its members, and has been in touch with similar groups in other countries. We have reason to believe that a sense of consternation has seized them, too, when reading the newspaper accounts of whatever happened last June in Turin. They, too, as some of the letters indicate, are wondering whether any forthcoming examination of the Shroud will again be held in secrecy, without taking into account suggestions that might come from experts throughout the world.

I may add that they ask pointedly whether the responsible authorities have given any thought to forming a really international commission that will suggest the best possible procedure, the best technical means for a thorough and definitive examination of the Shroud. For all who have the cause of the Relic at heart are anxious that the word that will come from a forthcoming examination be indeed final and conclusive.

Respectfully,

(Rev.) Peter M. Rinaldi, S.D.B.

The letter was not published in *Il Nostro Tempo*. Was it considered inopportune by the silent custodians of the Holy Shroud's citadel? Be it as it may, in a brief note from the editor, the writer was informed that the Turin weekly, in its February 15 edition, would publish an interview given by the Archbishop on the subject of the Shroud. "I trust," the editor concluded, "that you will find in it an authoritative reply to the questions you raised in your communication."

The unpublished "communication" eventually reached the Archbishop's desk. The Cardinal very kindly directed Monsignor Cottino, his delegate for the Shroud's affairs, to reply to the writer.

Gladly do I place myself at your disposal (Monsignor wrote) and at the disposal of the Holy Shroud Guild for whatever may develop with regard to the work of the Commission. Likewise, the Commission will be informed of your suggestion that members of the U.S. Guild be allowed to collaborate with the Commission's members.

On June 13, 1970, the unpublished letter to *Il Nostro Tempo* appeared in *The Tablet,* the leading English Catholic weekly, as part of an article written by Dr. David Willis, England's foremost medical authority on the Holy Shroud. Dr. Willis fully endorsed the letter. He is convinced, and stated it forthrightly in his article, that the unwarranted secrecy that surrounded the examination of the Shroud In June, 1969, "played into Herr Berna's hands and permitted him, without a shred of justification, to pillory both the Cardinal and the Vatican. The world press has been even more inept and allowed itself to be taken for a ride by a naïve visionary."

Dr. Willis hopes that the Turin authorities "will resist all temptation to secrecy and insist on a full-scale, open, legally attested, international, scientific investigation." He concludes:

To carry conviction the investigating experts must be internationally acknowledged and be chosen solely for their expertise in the relevant disciplines, quite independently of their nationality, or religious persuasions. Truth will only be served if Turin follows the highest traditions of the Lourdes Medical Bureau.[42]

These words of Dr. Willis are greeted by the friends of the Shroud with a fervent and resounding "Amen!"

CHAPTER EIGHT

A VOICE THROUGH THE CURTAIN OF SILENCE

Nearly eight months after the secret examination of the Holy Shroud held in June, 1969, Michele Cardinal Pellegrino, Archbishop of Turin, clarified the facts surrounding the event. A clarification was long overdue. The press communiqués had made a shambles of the case, intermingled as they were with Berna propaganda. The issue became so confused that not even a brief and rather noncommittal communiqué from the Vatican had helped to clarify it.

On February 15, 1970, the Turin Catholic weekly *Il Nostro Tempo* gave a full-page coverage to the long-awaited statement of Turin's Archbishop under the headline: *Un Mistero Chiamato Sindone* (A Mystery Called Shroud). It was actually an interview given by Cardinal Pellegrino to Paul Gilles, a reporter from Radio Luxembourg. Monsignor José Cottino, the Cardinal's delegate for the Shroud's affairs, and Monsignor Pietro Frutaz, undersecretary of the Vatican's Congregation for the Cause of Saints, an expert on relics, were also present.

At the outset of the interview, Cardinal Pellegrino stated that the primary purpose of the examination had been to ascertain the condition of the Shroud, and to see what measures might be taken to further preserve it against possible damage from the smog so prevalent in Turin. The Shroud was examined by experts in archaeology, chemistry, physiology and medicine "whose names are not at present revealed in order to shield them from the kind of publicity that would rather hinder than favour their researches".

The Shroud was found to be in good condition, actually in no way different than it had appeared when seen at the last exposition. The Cardinal stated that the experts came to no definite conclusions in their evaluation, "since much more time will be required for in-depth examinations which are to follow in the near future". Photographs were made using equipment far superior to that used nearly forty years ago. "These new photographs," the Archbishop remarked, "have given interesting results. However, these preliminary viewings must be followed by scientific tests which I believe will greatly contribute to the verification of the Shroud's authenticity. I do not think that it is possible, at this moment, to foresee what the over-all results will be."

The Cardinal brushed aside Berna's oft-repeated charge that the Vatican wants the Shroud's destruction on the grounds that the Relic proves that Christ was alive when laid in the sepulchre. "The Vatican," he said, "is very much interested in the Shroud, anxious, too, that it be preserved in the best possible way, and that these examinations be pursued with great care." He then mentioned the reasons behind the Holy See's official silence with regard to the authenticity of the Shroud. "The authenticity of a relic," he said, "is simply not within the scope of the Church's doctrinal definitions. We must note, too, that the historical documents supporting the Shroud are all too scarce. We hope, however, that new scientific evidence will permit us to make some very definite progress on the problem of the authenticity."

These are statements of a cautious man, a scholar in patristic theology and an expert in documentary Church history; evidently, too, a man who has not had the opportunity of evaluating the complexus of scientific problems implicit in the study of the Holy Shroud. This is all for the best

111

if it means that the Cardinal, under whose watchful eye the investigation is taking place, will see that every available scientific test will be made in the course of the Relic's examination.

In the closing statement of the Archbishop, the writer perceives more than just a trace of enthusiasm, quite unusual in the prelate's conversations on the subject of the Shroud prior to the June event. I am convinced that the scholarly Cardinal was much impressed with what he saw and heard in the course of the private examination of the Relic. After mentioning the fact that the mysterious body imprints on the Cloth are perfect negatives, something totally beyond the conception of people centuries ago, he speaks of the extraordinary coincidence of the traits of the image of the Shroud with the story of the Passion. He then concludes:

Finally there is that marvellous, truly noble and majestic Face which is revealed to us from the Shroud. No one with this in mind can be blamed for not taking the Turin Shroud lightly and not recognizing in it an extraordinary document of the Passion of Christ.[43]

A voice has finally spoken through the curtain of silence. The world now knows where the official Church stands with regard to the present and the future of Christianity's most prestigious Relic. Will the future justify the world's expectations?

EPILOGUE

As this monograph goes into its fourth printing (June, 1973), there is more than just a promise of action on the Holy Shroud front. The Church authorities in Turin have made no official announcement to date, but they have privately let it be known that a public exposition of the Shroud is being planned for the near future. Following the public viewing, a scientific examination of the Relic will be held by an international commission of experts now being formed.

Michele Cardinal Pellegrino, Archbishop of Turin and official custodian of the Shroud, in a letter to the writer dated May 8th, 1973, stated: "We are hard at work preparing for both the exposition and the scientific examination." The *New York Times*, on Easter Sunday of this same year, in a detailed article on the subject of the Shroud, confirmed what newspapers in Europe have stated in recent months, i.e., that "the Turin Relic will be the object of a new and definitive examination by experts in the fall". Headlined "SHROUD

OF TURIN FACING INQUIRY," the *New York Times* article stated: "The Shroud of Turin, venerated by some as the burial cloth of Jesus, may soon undergo an examination to determine its authenticity. A commitment has been made to show the much-guarded Easter Relic in public as a preliminary to the investigation by scientists."

While waiting for the Turin authorities to confirm officially their "commitment" to proceed with the historic event, believers in the authenticity are justifiably anxious to know what the new scientific examination will actually involve. Who are the "experts" called to examine the Relic? To what kind of tests will the Shroud be subjected? What results can be expected from this investigation? Will these results prove definitely that the Turin Relic is indeed the burial cloth of Jesus ?

The new examination, we are assured, will far exceed in scope and procedure the one held in the nineteen-thirties, and will cover the entire spectrum of disciplines relevant to the Shroud. The investigating experts are chosen solely on their expertise, independently of their nationality or religious persuasions. While this augurs well for the cause of the Relic, it would be foolhardy to think that the examination will once and for all solve all the enigmas of the Shroud. Like other students of the Relic, I am convinced that some of the tests will add new and surprising evidence in favour of the authenticity. But the Shroud presents such a unique complexus of incredible details and problems that even a most searching investigation may leave us with more than a few unanswered questions.

A case in point we have with regard to the bloodstains on the Cloth. While physiologists marvel at the realism of the stains and of the wounds that caused them (cf. p. 39), they have not been able thus far to determine if there is any trace of actual human blood on the Shroud. Testing by spectroscopy, programmed in the forthcoming examination, may prove the presence of human blood on the Cloth. But the opponents of the authenticity may well come back to us with a question which the spectroscopy test leaves unanswered: how do we know that it was Jesus' body that stained the Shroud?

The dating of the Cloth is essential to the problem of the Shroud. Textile experts have satisfactorily shown (cf. p. 58) that the Relic is identical in material and weave pattern to numerous fabrics from the Near East, dated reliably from the first century. But this does not satisfy some Shroud students who want the

Carbon 14 test applied to the Shroud. This test is more than a little questionable for a number of practical reasons which we enumerated on page 59, but even if it were applied with results favouring the authenticity (as was the case with the linen wrappings of the Dead Sea Scroll), the sceptic can always claim that the medieval artist who forged the Shroud used linen made in Palestine at the time of Christ.

Some experts believe that testing by infra-red photography might throw some light on the origin and nature of the incredible imprints on the Shroud. Others are not so sure. But however inconclusive this test, believers in the Relic's authenticity feel their questions are still valid. "Why is it," they ask, "that in all the history of pictorial art there is nothing that even approximates the images on the Shroud? Who was the superhuman genius who, centuries ago, conceived of and used the process that gave us those images? And how was he able to duplicate the conditions and unique circumstances of the Crucifixion reflected with uncanny realism in the picture of the anatomically perfect body of the Man of the Shroud?"

The scientists who will examine the Turin Relic—experts of international repute in archaeology, pictorial art, chemistry, physiology and related sciences—will render a most useful service to the cause of the Shroud even if they will not have an answer to every question posed by the ancient linen. Believers in its authenticity are convinced that the new findings will not only confirm the previous ones, but will bring new light on many debated points; enough to prove that, in the case of the Shroud, we are dealing with a truly unique object before which even the most hardened sceptic will do well to pause and think.

In the course of his lectures to rapt audiences who never tire of the Passion story as the Shroud tells it, the writer has often remarked that the best things about the Holy Shroud have yet to be told. Some of them will undoubtedly come to light during the forthcoming examination. But I am also convinced that this new investigation, rather than say the last word, will lay the groundwork for even more astonishing revelations to come in the future. As I ask the reader to join me in a prayer that this may indeed come to pass, let me invite him to ponder the words of a man who wrote about the Shroud in a far better way than I ever hope to do.

Should we not consider the Shroud of Turin as a gift to our century? It was photography that detected for us, in the negative image, the magnificient image of the Lord, latent in the Cloth. Only modern and especially scientific investigation has been able to throw light on this unique and so disputed Relic, and to guarantee its authenticity. For the science-conscious man of today, we have opened a new and signally appropriate approach to Jesus Christ.[44]

BIBLIOGRAPHY

The items listed comprise the most important works on the Holy Shroud in English since the Relic's exposition in 1931. For more extensive bibliographies in English as well as in other languages, see Bulst, Walsh and Wuenschel, below.

Books and Pamphlets

Barbet, Pierre, *A Doctor at Calvary*, Dublin, 1953.

Barnes, Arthur, *The Holy Shroud of Turin*, London, 1934.

Bulst, Werner, *The Shroud of Turin*, Milwaukee, 1957.

Cheshire, Capt. G., *Pilgrimage to the Shroud*, New York, 1956.

Hyneck, Rudolph, *The True Likeness*, New York, 1951.

Rinaldi, Peter, *I Saw The Holy Shroud*, Tampa, 1940.

Walsh, John, *The Shroud*, New York, 1963.

Weyland, Peter, *A Sculptor Interprets the Holy Shroud*, Esopus, New York, 1954.

Wuenschel, Edward, *Self-portrait of Christ*, Esopus, 1954.

Articles

Abbott, Walter, "The Shroud and the Holy Face", *American Ecclesiastical Review,* CXXXII (1955).

Bucklin, Robert, "The Medical Aspects of the Crucifixion", *Linacre Quarterly*, February, 1958.

Green, Maurus, O.S.B., "Enshrouded in Silence", *Ampleforth Journal,* LXXIV (Autumn, 1969).

Meyer, Karl E., "Were you there when they photographed my Lord", *Esquire,* August, 1971.

O'Gorman, P. W., "The Holy Shroud of Jesus Christ", *American Ecclesiastical Review,* CII (1940).

Rinaldi, Peter, "The Holy Shroud", *Sign Magazine,* 1934.

Sava, Anthony, "The Wounds of Christ", *Catholic Biblical Quarterly,* XVI (1954).

Willis, David, "Did He die on the Cross?", *Ampleforth Journal,* LXXIV (Spring, 1969).

Vignon, P., and Wuenschel, E., "The Problem of the Holy Shroud", *Scientific American,* XCIII (1937).

Wuenschel, Edward, "The Holy Shroud", *American Ecclesiastical Review,* CII (1940).

Wuenschel, Edward, "The Truth about the Holy Shroud", *American Ecclesiastical Review*, CXXIX (1953).

NOTES

1. J. Walsh, *The Shroud,* New York, 1963, Preface.
2. Cf. *The Catholic Encyclopedia* (1913): Troyes, Diocese of, Vol. 15, p. 67.
3. Riant, *Exuviae sacrae Constantinopolitanae,* II, p. 232.
4. Duchesne, *Histoire de l'Eglise de Besançon,* Paris, 1909, p. 69.
5. J. Walsh, *op. cit.,* p. 50 ff, and 112 ff.
6. P. Barbet, *Les Cinq Plaies du Christ,* Paris, 1935, p. 87.
7. J. Walsh, *op. cit.,* p. 133.
8. P. Barbet, *A Doctor at Calvary,* Dublin, 1953, p. 183.
9. *Ibid,* p. 185.
10. A. S. Barnes, *The Holy Shroud of Turin,* London, 1934, p. 89 ff.
11. Cf. E. Levesque, "Le Suaire de Turin et l'Evangile", *Nouvelle Revue Apologétique,* Paris, 1939.
12. *Ibid.*
13. U. Chevalier, *Etude Critique sur l'origine du Saint Suaire,* Paris, 1900.
14. W. Bulst, S.J., *The Shroud of Turin,* Milwaukee, 1956, p. 28.
15. *Ibid,* p. 29.
16. J. Walsh, *op. cit.,* p. 170.
17. W. Bulst, S.J., *op. cit.,* p. 30.
18. P. Vignon and E. Wuenschel, "The Problem of the Holy Shroud", *Scientific American,* March, 1937, p. 162.

19. *Ibid.*
20. Quoted by D. Willis in his article "Did He Die on the Cross?," *Ampleforth Journal,* London, (Spring, 1969.)
21. P. Barbet, *A Doctor at Calvary,* p. 9.
22. *Ibid*, p. 26.
23. *Ibid*, p. 27.
24. W. Bulst, *op. cit.,* p. 54.
25. *Ibid*, p. 55.
26. *Ibid,* p. 71.
27. P. Barbet, *A Doctor at Calvary,* p. 73.
28. A. Sava, "The Wound in the Side of Christ", *Catholic Biblical Quarterly,* Vol. XIX, No. 3 (July, 1957) pp. 343-346.
29. From H. Mödder's address to the International Sindonological Congress, Rome, 1950, *Acts of the Congress,* Turin, 1951.
30. D. Willis, *op. cit.,* p. 7.
31. C. Fouard, *The Christ the Son of God,* Chicago, 1927, p. 379.
32. Quoted by R. W. Hyneck in the *Rivista dei Giovani,* Turin, April 1935, p. 47.
33. F. R. Von Lama, *Therese Neumann,* New York, 1931, p. 107.
34. W. Bulst, *op. cit.,* p. 104.
35. L. Fossati, *Conversazioni e discussioni sulla Santa Sindone,* Turin, 1968, p. 59.
36. G. Ricci, *L'Uomo della Sindone e' Gesu',* Assisi, 1969, p. 278.
37. Quoted by P. M. Rinaldi, S.D.B., in *I Saw the Holy Shroud,* Tampa, 1940, p. 58.
38. P. Vignon, and E. Wuenschel, *loc. cit.*
39. W. Bulst, *op. cit.,* p. 27.
40. Maurus Green, O.S.B., "Enshrouded in Silence", *Ampleforth Journal,* Vol. LXXIV (Autumn, 1969), p. 343.
41. J. Walsh, *op. cit.,* p. 167.

42. D. Willis in *The Tablet,* London, June 13, 1970.
43. Michele Cardinal Pellegrino in *Il Nostro Tempo,* Turin, February 15, 1970.
44. W. Bulst, *op. cit.,* p. 110.